Carlo Acutis

Carlo Acutis

The First Millennial Saint

Nicola Gori

Translation by Daniel Gallagher

Our Sunday Visitor
Huntington, Indiana

Published in English by Our Sunday Visitor Publishing Division, Our Sunday Visitor, Inc., 200 Noll Plaza, Huntington, IN 46750; 1-800-348-2440; www.osv.com.

ISBN: 978-1-68192-935-4 (Inventory No. T2675)
1. Religion/Christianity/Saints & Sainthood
2. Biography & Autobiography/Religious
3. Religion/Christianity/Catholic

eISBN: 978-1-68192-936-1
LCCN: 2021934759

Cover design: Tyler Ottinger
Cover images: Photos Courtesy Carlo Acutis Center
Interior design: Amanda Falk
Interior art: Caroline Baker Mazure

PRINTED IN THE UNITED STATES OF AMERICA

CONTENTS

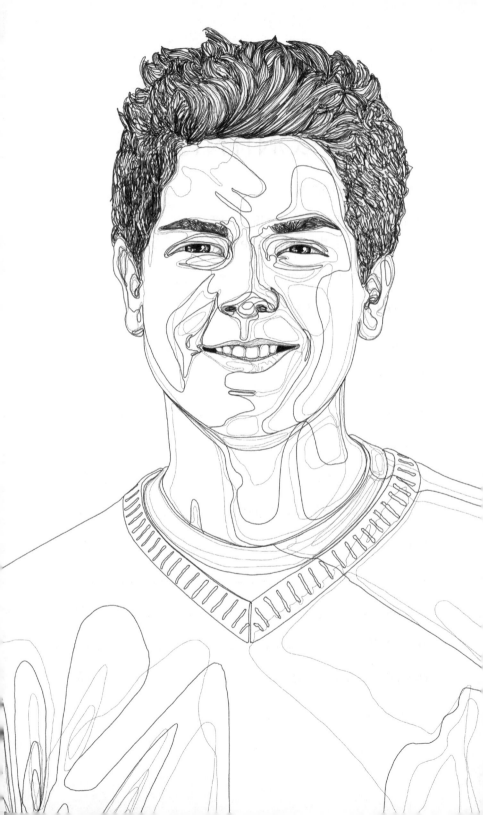

WORDS OF POPE FRANCIS

In his post-synodal apostolic exhortation to young people and the entire people of God entitled *Christus Vivit* (March 25, 2019), Pope Francis offered Carlo as an example of holiness to young people in the digital age. Pope Francis remarked that the internet can be risky, but it also has enormous potential. Carlo knew how to make the internet serve the common good and the Gospel, showing how to use it without compromising one's moral responsibilities. Carlo's knack for programming made him a pioneer and a model for every young person who uses computer technology. Pope Francis writes:

"I remind you of the good news we received as a gift on the morning of the Resurrection: that in all the dark and painful situations we have mentioned, there is a way out. For example, it is true that the digital world can expose you to the risk of self-absorption, isolation and empty pleasure.

But don't forget that there are young people even there who show creativity and genius. Such was the case with the Venerable Carlo Acutis.

"Carlo was well aware that the whole apparatus of communication, advertising, and social networking can be used to stupefy us, addict us to consumerism, and persuade us of the importance of having the latest gadget, to be obsessed with our free time, and to get caught up in negativity. Yet Carlo knew how to use communication technology to spread the Gospel and the values of goodness and beauty.

"Carlo didn't fall into the usual trap. He saw that many young people, wanting to be different, really end up being like everyone else, running after whatever those in power set before them with the mechanisms of consumerism and distraction. Thus, they do not bring to fruition the gifts that the Lord has given them. They fail to offer the world those unique, personal talents that God has given to each. As a result, Carlo said, 'Everyone is born original, but most end up dying photocopies.' Don't let this happen to you!

"Don't let them rob you of hope and joy, or drug you into becoming a slave to their interests. Dare to be more, because who you are is more important than any possession you own. What good are possessions or appearances? You can become what God your Creator knows you are, if only you realize that you are called to something greater. Ask the help of the Holy Spirit and confidently aim for the lofty goal of holiness. In this way, you will never become a photocopy. You will be fully yourself.

"If this is to happen, you need to realize one basic truth: being young is not only about pursuing fleeting pleasures and superficial achievements. If the years of your youth are to serve their purpose in life, they must become a time of generous commitment, whole-hearted dedication, and sacrifices that are difficult but ultimately fruitful."*

Pope Francis again drew attention to Carlo's life in his Angelus Address of October 11, 2020, the day after the beatification ceremony and a week after he had signed the encyclical *Fratelli Tutti* at the tomb of Saint Francis of Assisi:

"Yesterday, in Assisi, Carlo Acutis, a 15-year-old youth enamoured with the Eucharist, was beatified. He did not ease into comfortable inertia, but understood the needs of his time, because he saw the face of Christ in the weakest. His witness indicates to today's young people that true happiness is found by putting God in first place and serving Him in our brothers and sisters, especially the least. A round of applause for the new young Blessed!"†

---

* *Christus Vivit,* 104–108.
† Pope Francis, *Angelus,* October 11, 2020.

PREFACE:
IN THE FOOTSTEPS OF BLESSED CARLO ACUTIS ON THE PATH OF THE GOSPEL

"I remind you of the good news we received as a gift on the morning of the resurrection: that in all the dark or painful situations that we mentioned, there is a way out. For example, it is true that the digital world can expose you to the risk of self-absorption, isolation, and empty pleasure. But don't forget that there are young people even there who show creativity and even genius. That was the case with the Venerable Carlo Acutis. ... He knew how to use communications technology to transmit the Gospel, to communicate values and beauty."*

These are the words of Pope Francis who extolled the holiness of Carlo Acutis in *Christus Vivit,* addressed to "young people" and "the entire people of God." Carlo died from a sudden and violent illness in 2006 at the tender age of fifteen. In less than a decade, his story has had an enormous effect on the hearts of countless young people, communities, and youth groups in Italy and across the globe, both inside and outside the Catholic Church. Pope Francis declared him Venerable in 2018, opening the way to the beatification ceremony celebrated in Assisi on October 10, 2020. It was in Assisi — the earthy town of Saint Francis — a place he loved more than any other, a place he returned to repeatedly to refresh his soul, where Carlo was laid to rest.

Besides the usual things any teenager loves, Carlo had a deep and abiding love for the Eucharist: his "highway to heaven." His dedication to Mass, even when on vacation, demonstrates his awareness that it is precisely in the Eucharist that we experience our "memory of the future." The Eucharist, in fact, reveals that we are hidden with Christ in God (see Col 3:3), and by our participation in it, our fragile humanity gradually begins to show signs of its ultimate destiny: immersion in the life of the Trinity.

With this awareness, Carlo did not find meaning in life by seeking rewards or dreaming up futile projects, but — through his intelligence, his humanity, and his adolescent energy — by manifesting the life of God received through the gift of Baptism. This was the reason for his constant mantra to himself and his friends: "We are all born unique, but many die photocopies." As Pope Francis recalls in *Christus Vivit,* "Being young is not only about pursuing fleeting pleasures and superficial achievements. If the years of your youth are

---

Christus Vivit, 104–105.

to serve their purpose in life, they must be a time of generous commitment, whole-hearted dedication, and sacrifices that are difficult but ultimately fruitful."[†]

In the last moments of his life, Léon Bloy was fond of repeating, "There is only one sadness in life: not to be a saint." Pope Francis echoed these words in one of his early general audiences: "Let us not lose the hope of holiness, let us follow this path. Do we want to be saints? The Lord awaits us, with open arms; he waits to accompany us on the path to sanctity. Let us live in the joy of our faith, let us allow ourselves to be loved by the Lord."[‡]

This is exactly what this book is about. It is the story of a life utterly ordinary and unique — the life of Carlo Acutis — a life burning bright with the light of a God whose mystery nourished him in the Eucharist. It was precisely Carlo's unwavering devotion to the Eucharist that inspired him to tell the story of Eucharistic miracles through a website he created just for fun. He was eager to deepen his knowledge of these phenomena and strengthen his devotion to Jesus. The website subsequently caught the attention of people across the globe.[§] Thanks to the internet, his virtual Eucharistic miracle project spread to many countries and was translated into several languages. Through these stories, young people were introduced to the importance of recognizing and venerating the shrines of Eucharistic miracles.

Carlo Acutis was indeed an extraordinary young man, but, as his family — especially his mother Antonia — says, "in the end, it is not about Carlo, but Jesus. If Carlo can serve as an example of how to encounter Jesus, so be it." Antonia is the kind of mother who never tires talking about how sol-

---

[†] *C V,* 108.

[‡] Pope Francis, *General Audience,* October 2, 2013.

[§] See Miracolieucaristici.org.

id and clear her son's relationship with the Faith was, even though he lived it in a way any boy could. "Carlo noticed how kids would stand in line for hours to attend a concert of their favorite pop star, but in front of the tabernacle they felt nothing. We are indeed more fortunate than those who lived at the time of Jesus, because we can go out the front door and down the street to the nearest church to visit 'Jerusalem.' Carlo really wanted people to recognize this supreme gift. God is with us, and that reality should fill each and every one of us with hope and joy, even when we are hanging on the cross, because, as Carlo said, 'we all have to climb Golgotha.' All of us can be sanctified in the ascent."*

Carlo Acutis cultivated the beauty of a holiness implanted deep in the heart where God's voice calls us to trust the Spirit who gives us the wisdom to discern our chosen path, even in the exploding world of the internet. He was a computer whiz and a programming prodigy, so he clearly understood that holiness cannot be found if we cower in a corner, but only if we joyfully accept each day, give without counting the cost, and flee the temptation to think that our holiness can only be found in a single way of life or that the Christian life is merely a habit. Carlo was never satisfied with mediocrity, so he placed the most important reality at the center of his life: the Word of God and the Bread of Life.

Eucharist, charity, study, and the Rosary. Through these, the computer became Carlo's powerful instrument for evangelization. They turned this fifteen-year-old into the patron of the web and protector of all internet users. He was just as crazy about the internet as his peers, but only insofar as it would become a "vehicle for evangelization and catechesis."

Fifteen years don't seem like much, but, as Carlo demon-

---

* R. Benotti, *Carlo Acutis e l'autostrada per il Cielo. Parla la mamma: "Voleva che le persone capissero l'importanza dell'Eucarestia"*, Agenzia SIR, 12 gennaio 2019.

strates, they were enough for him to develop a deeper faith life than most adults. Holiness was the refrain of Carlo's life. It was his goal and the thing that made him a little "different" at school, in the pizzerias, and on the soccer field. He did not keep his "holiness kit" to himself, but freely shared it with others, explaining that it included an enormous desire to be holy, the willingness to attend Mass, receive Holy Communion, pray a daily Rosary, read a portion of the Bible, participate in Eucharistic adoration and sacramental confession, and cultivate a spirit of self-sacrifice to help others.

For Carlo, it was normal to seek friends in heaven. This is why he included a section on his webpage called "Discover how many friends you have in heaven." Users could learn about "young" saints: those who had reached their goal in record time. He himself was also convinced that he would not live to see old age. "I will die young," he often said. But in the meantime, he filled every day with a whirlwind of activity: teaching catechism, spending time with the poor at the soup kitchen, and chatting with kids at the youth group. Between one commitment and another, Carlo also found time to play the saxophone, soccer, and video games; watch his favorite police films; and make short films with his star cast of cats and dogs. Amid all this, he found time to keep up with studies at Leo XIII High School in Milan.

Speaking about the saints of every time and age, Pope Francis emphasized that they are similar to us. "In the faces of the humblest and least of our brothers, the smallest and most despised brothers, they saw the face of God, and now they contemplate him face to face in his glorious beauty. ... They are people who, before reaching the glory of heaven, lived normal lives with joys and sorrows, struggles and hopes."[†] These are the saints who live next door: people who have placed them-

---

† Pope Francis, *Angelus*, November 1, 2013.

selves at the service of the Gospel and whose extraordinary lives are lived in ordinary circumstances.

Carlo Acutis fully embraced the gift of God's life in baptism. By knowing how to participate in the very life of God, he was rendered capable of living the Faith not as an achievement of something unattainable, but as an acceptance of the manifestation of God's love. This is how his charity toward the poor in Milan and the quality of his relationship with friends at school became not only good works but opportunities to manifest — through his own humanity, intelligence, affectivity, and psychology — the very love of the Father. Even his interest in the internet was a way for him to witness to the love of God that transcends every border, language, and culture.

Just as Pope Francis emphasized in the encyclical *Fratelli Tutti* which he signed at Assisi, in today's world, "digital connectivity is not enough to build bridges. It is not capable of uniting humanity." What we really need is "physical gestures, facial expressions, moments of silence, body language and even the smells, the trembling of hands, the blushes and perspiration that speak to us and are a part of human communication."* This is the lesson Blessed Carlo teaches us: The internet and the digital word are precious commodities, but what we really need is a willingness to witness. What really counts is the love of the Father who transforms us and makes our lives a precious gift worth living fully to the very end.

Msgr. Dario E. Viganò
Vice-Chancellor of the Pontifical Academy of Sciences
and Social Sciences

---

* *Fratelli Tutti,* 43.

SILENCE: SPACE FOR PRAYER

Everything of value is born out of silence. Nothing could be more certain. But what is silence? It is difficult to say, because silence itself doesn't say anything to us. Only by experiencing it are we able to understand what it is and why it is important.

There are moments when silence is an atmosphere that surrounds and penetrates our innermost being, giving us a sense of fullness, not of emptiness; of presence, not of absence. Who has not tried to find it on the outside, in an open field, on a mountaintop at dawn or sunset, or under the starry skies at night? Everything is suspended in a silence pulsating with life, a silence in which we can perceive the harmony of the cosmos. This is, in a certain way, the experience of God's presence.

This experience can also be had simply by entering a deserted church and gazing at the tabernacle, whose lamp tells us that Jesus is truly present in the Eucharist. In silence we communicate with a "Thou" that is truly present through a condescension of overpowering love that touches us to the core and fills us with deep emotion, gratitude, and holy joy.

This was precisely Carlo Acutis's experience, who from the time of his first Communion made the Eucharist the center of his life. Or rather, he made it a privileged encounter with his friend Jesus, whom he was convinced was fully present to the world in the Eucharist in the same way he was present when he walked with the apostles and disciples.

Carlo took his studies seriously and cultivated many friendships. He was always going out with his friends and maintaining a busy schedule. But he always had time for his first priority: the Eucharist. Mass was an essential part of his daily routine, as was Eucharistic adoration. His devotion to the Eucharist turned him into the "meek lamb" who was his model. Without even realizing it, Carlo learned the meaning of true silence, which is a constant "yes" to God's will without rebellion or explanations. Silence is simply an embrace of God's love.

It is interesting to note that the first gift Carlo received from his mother was a little lamb with a thick coat of white wool. It was one of his most cherished possessions. This is significant because on the day of his first Communion, Carlo came across a little lost lamb along the road, almost as if it were a sign of what awaited him and a symbol of his life. Carlo himself became the Eucharist he received by offering himself in silence.

In his daily visits to the tabernacle — an appointment he never failed to keep — silence was precisely the way Carlo remained close to the heart of Jesus in his gift of self to the point of experiencing a complete unity with him. This is the mystical silence where divine love speaks to us more clearly.

Carlo was sociable and friendly with everyone he met. This characteristic was nourished especially in his intimate, silent encounters during which he experienced the Lord's goodness and joy and found the desire to share it with others. We could say that his interior beauty and his overflowing kindness and sympathy toward others were the fruit of spending time in loving silence with Jesus in Eucharistic adoration.

It is fair to say that every saint and towering human figure — be it in the arts or sciences — was formed in the school of silence. There Carlo learned to be quiet and to listen, to reflect and to meditate, searching humbly to know the truth.

If we are always immersed in noise and chatter, if we talk without thinking, we never become wise and mature. There is an old adage: "The wise man says few but well thought words. The chatterbox runs about in every direction."

Yet there is another kind of silence that is not so good; a silence that is not true silence, but merely the absence of sound. It is the kind of silence that divides; the kind of silence we feel when we are offended, or when we're unkind or showing we're simply not interested. It is an egocentric, non-Christian silence, because Jesus commands us to love everyone, even our enemies.

We must learn to tolerate even our enemies. Carlo gives us an example in this as well.

Even though he died young, Carlo learned in the school of "offenses." For example, his peers would tease him for going to Mass every day, and for his unfashionable way of dressing. But, as usual, Carlo proved he was a diligent disciple who knew how to harvest good fruit from every situation. He knew how to keep quiet, not always feeling the need to defend himself, and to tolerate offenses. Even though he was "different," Carlo knew how to win the esteem and friendship of his peers as well as that of many adults. His life — not only his words — became an evangelizing force, even though he did not overlook the power of words; in fact, he sought to make the most of them, especially by using them in modern forms of communication.

Jesus himself, the Word of God incarnate, lived in the silence of humility and patient suffering. He made his life a living oblation, desiring only to communicate goodness and peace. He loved to pass the entire night in silent communion with the Father, drawing the words that he would say to his apostles so that they, in turn, might communicate them to the Church and to the world.

Mary, the Mother of Jesus — together with Saint Joseph, whom God chose as Protector of Mother and Child — are also ideal models of silent contemplation.

To discover the beauty of silence is to discover the key to growth in every virtue.

There is a kind of silence for every moment of our existence. There is a silence that helps us live our lives in simplicity and peace. There is the silence of joy, the silence of adoration, the silence of humility, the silence in temptation, the silence that gives strength and faith, the silence that knows how to embrace suffering — physical or moral — without complaint or self-pity. This is what Sacred Scripture says: "Be still before the LORD; wait for him" (Ps 37:7). In the Hebrew text, "to be still" is the same verb used in Psalm 131 where the weaned child clings to its mother. This silence does not come to us automatically, and neither is it the result of heroic strength. It is a gift of the Holy Spirit. Carlo showed that he was full of it during the most excruciating moments of his illness when he accepted pain like the meek Lamb, allowing the Lord to bring his plan to completion within him. "In all my years," one of Carlo's nurses said, "I had never seen a patient undergo such sudden and extreme pain. It was incredible that he never complained, even with his legs and arms swollen to such proportions." Once when she asked him, "How are you feeling?", Carlo responded with his usual cheerfulness, "Well, as always!" Yet half an hour later he fell into a coma.

It has been said that Carlo Acutis departed for heaven "on eagle's wings." He could never have flown so high if he had not known how to say, in the hour of his deepest suffering, that he was "well" in a profound sense, because in the will of God one is always well. But where did his ability to say "yes, well!" come from? Undoubtedly from contemplation. He filled his soul and senses with God's peace by fixing his heart's gaze on heaven, listening to the music that can only be heard in the true silence of divine presence. Each and every one of us can and must harbor a place of "sacred silence," just as we experience in the liturgy.

In 1964, while Pope Saint Paul VI was on pilgrimage in the Holy Land, he recalled the life of the Holy Family in Nazareth. He said, "Above all, the Holy Family teaches us the value of silence. May we appreciate once again this marvelous and indispensable spiritual treasure, deafened as we are by so much tumult, so much noise, so many voices of our chaotic and frenzied modern life. O silence of Nazareth, teach us recollection, reflection, and eagerness to heed the good inspirations and words of true teachers; teach us the need and value of preparation, of study, of meditation, of interior life, of secret prayer seen by God alone."

This is all the more necessary in our time when silence has become almost impossible due to the noise of mass media and social and family life that is all exterior, superficial, and often alienating.

It is said that words are silver and silence is golden. A

person's weight — his value — is proportionate to his capacity for silence. True silence, in fact, gives room for the action of grace, to the guiding and soothing power of the Holy Spirit, the Spirit of truth and love, the Spirit of communion and peace, the Spirit of holiness and joy.

Mother Anna Maria Cànopi, OSB
Abbazia Benedettina "Mater Ecclesiæ"
Isola San Giulio Orta (Novara)

PREFACE TO THE NEW EDITION

There is a way to avoid the deadening of conscience that is so typical of our modern age. With an extraordinary witness in ordinary daily life, Blessed Carlo Acutis (1991–2006) shows us the way: Christ himself, who is the way, the truth, and the life. He shines as a light of holiness to people everywhere, no matter what their daily responsibilities are. Having lived only fifteen years on this earth, Carlo used that brief span of life to communicate a powerful message: Loved by the Father, each and every person has a unique role to play in his plan of salvation. Carlo was most famous for saying, "Everyone is born original, but most end up dying photocopies." This is the risk of not living life to the fullest but settling for models that undermine the authentic vocation we have received from God: namely, to seek our happiness in union with him.

Carlo has awakened our conscience to rediscover values that will never grow old: Most importantly, he proposed Christ as our form of life and hope. He has shown us that when we are in union with God, we can find true peace and the fulfillment of our deepest desires. The enduring truth of Carlo's message was affirmed by the Church when, on October 10, 2020, he was beatified in the Upper Basilica of Saint Francis of Assisi in a ceremony presided over by Cardinal Agostino Vallini, Pontifical Legate for the Basilicas of Saint Francis and Saint Mary of the Angels in Assisi.

So, what does it mean for Carlo to be Blessed? Essentially it means that the Church has recognized him as a model of holiness for all the faithful, and that he can be remembered in public liturgies such as the celebration of Mass in his honor and the dedication of chapels and altars in his name, even if his cult is not yet universal but limited to the Diocese of Assisi-Nocera Umbra-Gualdo Tadino and the Archdiocese of Milan.

And what are we to think of a beatification that echoed throughout the world due to extensive coverage in the media and social communications? In the first place, it affirms that Carlo speaks to the world in a simple, straightforward language that gets right to the point. Secondly, his witness attracts people of all ages, races, and languages. This is because wherever Carlo is, God is. Carlo is his messenger, his herald. The new Blessed offers people the joy of encountering Christ. Whenever Carlo spoke of himself, he indirectly spoke of God. This is why his beatification was celebrated with such joy and with a hymn of praise and thanks to the Lord for giving us this young man.

The miracle that paved the way for his beatification took place in Brazil. A young boy named Mattheus Vianna was afflicted with a serious birth defect called annular pancreas, causing him to vomit constantly, leading to serious malnutrition. The prognosis was not good. He needed to undergo major therapeutic surgery, but he was never able to do so. Medication had no effect on the pathology. The boy's healing started immediately after he had touched a relic of Blessed Carlo during the celebration of Mass at his parish on October 12, 2012, the anniversary of Carlo's death. His recovery was rapid and complete (i.e., functionally and anatomically), enduring, and scientifically inexplicable.

Now that he is beatified, Carlo has much to say to us. He shows us how to place God at the center of our lives, to comprehend that there is a reality beyond the perceivable material world: a world that projects into eternity. He has discovered that, even in our secularized society, there is another dimension to look forward to. Why are people turning to Carlo? Why is this simple teenager so popular? I think the answer is found in the concrete nature of his evangelical witness. People perceive him as a friend, a companion for the journey, an adolescent who lived life with eyes turned toward heaven and his feet on the ground, helping others in any way he could. He began with the poorest and those most in need. Following the example of Saints Francis of Assisi and Anthony of Padua, Carlo found his worth in giving away not only material goods, but the goods of the heart. He made an integral offering of himself, uniting his person to Christ sacrificed for the whole human race. Was the Eucharist not his primary devotion? Is his best-known motto not "The Eucharist is my highway to heaven"? Wherever Carlo is, Emmanuel is, "God-with-us." Carlo proclaims to his contemporaries that Christ is present in our lives; he is a reality to be taken seriously because he is closer to us than we can ever imagine. With his witness, Blessed Carlo affirms that Jesus is by our side at every moment. This certitude of

God's presence was reflected in his behavior towards others in which we clearly see the face of Christ. Praise to the Eucharistic Lord and service to the neediest are two sides of the same coin, for both are rooted in charity without limits. Passionately in love with God, Carlo's heart beat in unison with those who suffer. We will never understand Carlo fully until we understand this. And this is perhaps what fascinates people the most and attracts them to know more about the Blessed. He is brimming with sympathy, precisely because of his open frankness in witnessing to the love of God. He does it with sympathy and complete coherence between the Creed he professed and his way of life. The strength of his proclamation was in his willingness to open himself to the breath of the Holy Spirit.

Carlo is God's invitation to run to him in these difficult times. People sense that there is an underlying reality to Carlo, a presence and an ecclesial communion that supports him. He is a son of the Church, an expression of the universal call to holiness. He embodies the fragility of adolescence and creation, but also the strength of grace that transformed him into an everlasting praise to God's glory.

Carlo is also a shining witness to the Christian Faith, the first seeds of which were implanted by a Polish babysitter who taught him not only the rudiments of Catholicism, but also prayer. There is a powerful lesson in this: The laity have an enormous responsibility and role in passing on the Faith. Carlo's life affirms this. It is astounding to think that it was not primarily Carlo's birth-family who initially taught him how to live according to the precepts of the Gospel. It was rather he who pulled his family along in the journey of faith. This is an important factor to keep in mind if we are to comprehend Blessed Carlo's ability to attract so many people to God.

We know that his journey to holiness began at a tender age. He was a kid just like any other, but he did have a particular curiosity in the Bible, the *Catechism of the Catholic Church*, and the lives of the saints. He was fascinated by stories of Our Lady's apparitions at Fatima, Lourdes, and Guadalupe. He was deeply devoted to the Virgin Mary and recited the Rosary every day because he considered it the greatest opportunity to spend time with the primary female figure in his life. The search for traces of God's self-manifestation in history gave Carlo the opportunity to reflect on God's mercy, his providence, and his desire to save all creatures.

Carlo considered Marian apparitions to be a sign of Mary's maternal care for her children. He also considered it a tangible expression of the Father's love and care for all humanity. A sense of God's fatherhood and his care for even the smallest of creatures is strongly present in Carlo's life. He learned from Saint Francis to love the least, the marginalized, the excluded, and those whom society considers "non-essential." Carlo learned to recognize the human dignity of every person he encountered along the way, regardless of religion or nationality.

Carlo's openness to others, his willingness to accept surprises, and his delight in diversity made him a citizen of the world. No culture was foreign to him, no ethnicity unworthy of forming a close friendship with. He was always ready to discuss important issues, seeing God's hand in current events. He learned to recognize God's presence in his brothers and sisters. He discovered a God who called him to service. Carlo was open to the promptings of the Holy Spirit because he was never closed in on himself. There was no room for self-centeredness in his heart. His capacity to perceive signs of God's will in everything happening around him was one of his most outstanding personal traits. It allowed him to direct his attention to those situations where a bit of charity was needed. He felt enveloped in this charity, and he was willing to bet his very existence on it. His charity was simply a reflection of his love for Jesus. It was an imperishable love; a love that could only grow in intensity over time. Those around him were constantly amazed at his capacity to give of himself. He not only rushed to help any of his schoolmates in need but tried to make himself all things to all men in imitation of his model: Christ, the Lamb of God. Thus, it is not surprising that so many people are fascinated by his example and seek his help and support through prayer to confront daily challenges and find direction in prayer and spirituality.

Ever since his death, people have spontaneously invoked his help with the sure hope that they would be heard. There are numerous testimonies of graces received through his intercession. What is most impressive is that those who seek his assistance are of no single class, language, or culture. Even non-Catholics turn to him. Why is there so much trust in this young man? Why is devotion to him so widespread? Perhaps because he speaks for the young generation. He knew their language. He used the same social media platforms they did, the same smartphones. He demystified the world of digital devices and computers since he was a genius with them. No area of modern communications was foreign to him. This is another reason why young people are so strongly attracted to him and consider him a big brother in the Faith. But there is more behind his gifts of communication that draw throngs of people to rediscover Christ. His secret is that he communicates a Person. He is the spokesperson for the One who can save us, body and soul. Carlo thus renews our nostalgia for the Creator. Unconsciously we seek a person just as Carlo did, because in the depths of our heart we need God, his love, and his mercy. Carlo is his mediator, a herald announcing that we need to make space for the Lord.

In Carlo, Jesus loves all young people in the world, and in him all young people are reflected as loved by God. They understand that a life like Carlo's is an assurance that they too can find redemption and peace. The love of Christ surrounding Carlo reverberated in every person he came into contact with. The closer we approach Carlo, the more we feel that he wants us to encounter God. Is it not this pull toward the Absolute that brought him to discover the riches of the Eucharist? In the Eucharist, he found the answer to all his questions about the meaning of life. He felt that Jesus is always among us. He is closer to us than we could ever imagine. He has pitched his tent among us.

This is the force behind a question Brother Matteo posed to Francis of Assisi about the fame and popularity that surrounded him: "Why is the whole world seeking you out? Why does it appear that everyone wants to see you, hear you, obey you? Why, Francis?" What pressed so many people to seek out the Saint, to meet him, to want to speak with him, and to follow him? It had to have been his simplicity, poverty, frankness, and closeness to the lowliest.

These are the same things we find fascinating about Carlo, who joined the saints in betting his entire life on Christ, thus discovering the joy of friendship with him. This also explains the choice of placing the mortal remains of Carlo in the Shrine of the *spogliazione* or "stripping" where Francis shed the clothes of a rich man and put on the cloak of evangelical poverty. This evangelical radicalness was also characteristic of Carlo when he affirmed that he "always wanted to be united with Christ."

Another common element between them is the love of the Eucharist. In the Eucharist, the Poverello (Francis of Assisi's nickname) saw God's humility in becoming man among us, and Carlo saw the "highway to heaven." These are, in fact, two sides of the same coin, just as the two of them shared a great devotion toward the Virgin Mary and the option of poverty as a privileged way of loving Christ. Francis and Carlo were two apostles who sought to invite their brothers and sisters into the adventure of the spirit, albeit in different times and circumstances, but nonetheless with the same interior strength that made them heralds of the Gospel. For Carlo, this involved the new frontier of information technology, where there was a greater need for God than ever.

In particular, Carlo gives an example to young people by instilling in their hearts a desire to open themselves to Christ, because in him we see a clear example of how beautiful and joyful it is to live for the Gospel. There is nothing sad about forming a friendship with God. Another aspect to consider is that Carlo, even though he came from a well-to-do family, did not consider the same things that other people consider indispensable, such as an abundance of material goods and a lot of money. Carlo considered these secondary and easy to forgo in the face of friendship with Christ.

Blessed Carlo also never hid his preference for the things of God. In this way, he opened himself up to holiness, but he did so without a hint of sadness or any suggestion that they did not bring joy. And this indeed is an important message for young people, because it shows that a relationship with Jesus is essentially a fountain of joy. Another important lesson that Carlo left for young people is how to die. After having lived his life in a close relationship with Christ, rooted in his love and the mystery of faith, when he finally met Sister Death, he accepted it with tranquility, knowing full well that she never has the last word.

These are the reasons why Carlo's memory is so alive in the hearts of so many people; because no one can remain indifferent in the face of a teenager so open to the Absolute, so ready to speak of God as a real person with whom he cultivated a real relationship. With his beatification, the Church offers his example to the world as a witness to Christ, proposing it as a model of charity, faith, and trust in God. Carlo basically teaches us that holiness is not a privileged state for a particular age, but that it is open to people of any culture, race, language, and at any time in life.

Nicola Gori

INTRODUCTION

"To always be united with Christ: This is my life's program."
Impressive words for a fifteen-year-old. His name was Carlo Acutis. Born to an Italian family in London, he spent his brief time on this earth like so many young people of his generation, involved with games, school, sports, computers, friends, and animals — especially dogs for which he had a great passion. But in the midst of a life so similar to his peers, there was something different: his extraordinary friendship with Jesus. This was Carlo's secret!

It was precisely an encounter with Christ that characterized this young man who lived a simple, coherent, joyous faith.

If we fail to recognize this Christological dimension, we fail to explain the whole of Carlo's life, and we will completely fail to understand what was going on in the depths of his soul. To be a kid like any other kid means to live in the company of friends, to joke around with them, to hang out in the school halls with them, and to run through the streets of your neighborhood with them. Today, it also means to play with the technological toys that have come to define a generation. It also means to come up with grand plans for the future with the boundless energy typical of that age. It is clear that Carlo lived every moment of his life intensely, but without ever excusing himself from his duties. Despite the small trials that come in any adolescent's life, he confronted everything with optimism and joy and always had the other person as his main interest. Perhaps it was this great love and interest in his neighbors that attracted everyone to him, even when he was still a baby. Every personal encounter was an important event for Carlo, for he saw in the other person an image of the God whom he loved so deeply. Into this rich, variegated, and fragmented life, Carlo inserted the presence of Christ, whom Carlo accepted with his entire will and desire to do good.

This is how Carlo's parish priest, Monsignor Gianfranco Poma, pastor of Santa Maria Segreta in Milan, spoke of him: "Carlo was unforgettable. My recollection of him is as clear as day. I could describe him to a T. Above all was his face: so honest and open. His face alone was simply a great big smile to life. It was the face of a boy with nothing to hide and a burning desire to communicate. I can still hear the tone of his voice as he tells stories or asks questions about this or that. His voice was always clear with nothing to hide; a voice that always wanted to run his thoughts and plans for the future by you. I remember clearly his observations, discussions, and the opinions he would share with me every once in a while. He never gave airs but was also never timid."

In his testimony, Monsignor Poma also points to particular traits in Carlo's spiritual life and personality. "He had the gift of a concrete and persuasive temperament. He was always aware that there was a tomorrow, and he was always discreet. This is perhaps what I remember most about Carlo. I would add that this dear image of Carlo has always had — and still has — the power to assuage the pain that he is no longer with me, my staff, and the entire parish community; the pain of having to say "goodbye" to him so suddenly. We were so dismayed in the face of a loss so unexpected and upsetting. As I remember him now as a presence that has never ceased to be with us, I have to ask myself: What gift does God continue to give in him?

Carlo was such a manifest grace in our lives, a sign that it was not difficult for a lively and healthy boy to combine the Gospel and celebration, moral uprightness with good humor, intelligence, and amiability. Carlo was so sweetly naïve of his exceptional personal qualities in every dimension of his daily life: at home, at school, at catechesis, in friendships, and in his relationship with God. He was generous with everyone and took no offense with anyone. He was always so polite, even though he was firmly planted in his convictions."

In his human and priestly experience, Monsignor Poma was able to affirm with certainty that Carlo was "a flesh-and-blood example of well-roundedness in the depth of his person and on every level of his life. He was without pretense, able to express himself and to listen, never judgmental of anyone, and never giving a thought to showing off or taking credit. He did not give the impression of living a brilliant life, but he did give the impression of living life fully and intensely. He didn't walk around like a 'little saint' if by this we mean something artificial, inauthentic, and foreign to the rest of his life. He was entirely transparent, never brooding but always bubbling with boundless interests. Whenever you met him, you might stop to chat for a moment, and you came away with the impression that he was someone who not only enjoyed his own life, but the lives of others, always with wit and true respect. He never gave the impression that he was guarding himself to make sure that he would always be a good boy and never mess up. To the contrary, he was always engaged in lively discussions with himself about everything he noted in his activities and in the lives of those with whom he lived and shared his daily rhythm. 'I love to talk with Jesus about everything I am experiencing and feeling.' When he told me this, I realized it was the secret of the purity of his soul and of his frankness."

Because of his intimate knowledge of Carlo, Monsignor Poma is an excellent source for Carlo's other notable qualities: "Whenever I talked with him and listened to him talk about what was going on in his life and what he was searching for, I could tell that Carlo had a very lively personality, but not frenetic, distracted, or restless. He loved to recollect in the depths of his soul and immerse himself in conversations with God. He was always faithful to this; it was his method of not sinking into ideas that were too abstract about what was happening around him. He often concluded conversations with a quick 'the Lord will surely come.' I don't know in detail what his 'devotions' were (he was always wary of boasting of his spiritual secrets). But I can certainly attest to his intense relationship with the Eucharist."

Monsignor Poma is convinced that Carlo is not a lost friend, but a spiritual companion who will never leave his side. He senses Carlo's invitation to hand on the precious inheritance he left for his fellow teens: "I often sense that he is right next to me, encouraging me with his smile, especially when something is bothering me or when I have questions about how to best lead the youth spiritually. When I think of him and his simple straightforwardness, I remind myself that the Lord offers grace in unforeseeable ways. Carlo taught me that a grace is not truly a grace if one feels the need to boast about it. This is precisely how it was with Carlo. He was a true Christian boy."

The life of Carlo is a perfect affirmation of the truth of the universal call to holiness. Pope Francis elaborated on this call in his general audience of November 19, 2014: "First of all, we must bear clearly in mind that sanctity is not something we can procure for ourselves, that we can obtain by our own qualities and abilities. Sanctity is a gift, it is a gift granted to us by the Lord Jesus, when He takes us to Himself and clothes us in Himself, He makes us like Him." In fact, "sainthood truly is the most beautiful face of the Church, the most beautiful face: it is to rediscover oneself in communion with God, in the fullness of his life and of his love. Sanctity is understood, then, not as a prerogative of the few: sanctity is a gift offered to all, no one excluded, by which the distinctive character of every Christian is constituted."

Pope Francis continues: "All this makes us understand that, in order to be saints, there is no need to be bishops, priests or religious: no, we are all called to be saints! ... Many times we are tempted to think that sainthood is reserved only to those who have the opportunity to break away from daily affairs in order to dedicate themselves exclusively to prayer. But it is not so! Some think that sanctity is to close your eyes and to look like a holy icon. No! This is not sanctity!" In fact, "sanctity is something greater, deeper, which God gives us. Indeed, it is precisely in living with love and offering one's own Christian witness in everyday affairs that we are called to become saints. And each in the conditions and the state of life in which he or she finds him- or herself." These words make it clear enough that everyone is called to holiness without distinction of race, language, age, or culture.

Christ's invitation to holiness is for every human creature! It is up to us to accept it with joy and to support it in one another since, as Pope Francis says, "the path to sainthood is not taken alone, each one for oneself, but is traveled together, in that one body that is the Church, loved and made holy by the Lord Jesus Christ."

Carlo, even though he never heard this catechesis, knew it subconsciously from his childhood, and he put it into practice. He had a natural experience of this union with Christ as if it were something quotidian, spontaneous, for in his innocence, he believed that other creatures must have had the same experience.

Holiness was simply a way of life for Carlo. Even though it cost him a great deal of sacrifice, it was connatural to him. For Carlo, "holiness is not a process of adding anything, but of subtraction. It is a removal of myself to make space for God." He lived this union with God with ease and evangelical simplicity. It emerged discretely in everything he did, without ostentation, but with a lightness — a frankness — that characterizes the souls of those who are very close to God. As Carlo gradually grew up, he began to show traits that revealed the spiritual depth of his being more and more. Even his schoolmates perceived something different in their friend. No one could really fully comprehend how deep Carlo's relationship with Christ was, but everyone knew it was there.

"Not I, but God." These words uttered by Carlo contain everything there is to know about his spiritual richness. He felt that he was a creature loved by God, and, at the same time, he felt the need to comprehend the role that Divine Providence has assigned to him. He was not only convinced that he needed to consider himself entirely dependent on God in every element of his existence, but he enjoyed this dependence that rendered him a true son of the merciful Father. In fact, he always found a way to put "God in place of himself." His every action reflected this principle. He lessened himself in order to let Christ grow and thus participate fully in the salvific plan that God had in mind for each and every person. Carlo used to say that God created time for us, and in the Incarnation, he assumed time into himself and sanctified it. In his daily habits, Carlo showed us how to live time without wasting it in things that displease God.

With regard to Carlo's use of time, Monsignor Poma wrote: "We all have some kind of calendar: in our pocket, on the wall, on our cell phone, or whatever. We all have one, and young people seem to start living by one earlier than ever before (think of a baby's schedule!) and maintaining one well into old age (think of our grandparents' calendar!). Our calendars get more and more stuffed. Most people simply couldn't survive without one. In fact, our schedules seem to have taken the place of diaries, which used to be so important. In fact, what is a school diary but an agenda — a list of 'things to do' at a certain time and in a certain place. If we read carefully, we see that the four Gospels also give us a sort of 'agenda' for Jesus, each in its own way."

Monsignor Poma explains that an agenda reminds us that "our lives are woven by actions and events, circumstances and responses, attempts and failures, pleasant and tiresome meetings we must absolutely keep. Our agendas, therefore, do say something about the extent to which we are living as Christians. Jesus showed us this in a most authoritative way. A 'Christian' agenda has this quality: Beside each reminder of something we have 'to do' (when, where, with whom, and why), there is a single page in which, for all the days of the year and of our lives, the same thing should be written over and over again: 'We have beheld his glory' (Jn 1:14)."

Monsignor Poma also recalls how one afternoon, he had an unforgettable conversation with Carlo precisely about his agenda. "He was listing and explaining the various appointments he had. It was clear this boy had a plethora of interests and many talents, but he was also someone who knew how not to become overwhelmed with a fragmentation of endless things just to keep busy. Jesus' response to his mother comes to mind: 'You do not know what I am about,' and it was not difficult for me to see that Carlo did not want to become disoriented and distracted from the things that really mattered in life. From that conversation, I remember the two pages of his agenda: On one side, his daily appointments, and on the other side, the phrase: 'We have seen his glory.' This was the page that kept an interminable smile on his face. The two facing pages were not opposed to each other, but neither could one substitute for the other. Rather, this biblical refrain entrusted, so to speak, all of Carlo's appointments, experiences, projects, and steps to achieve them into the hands of God in such a way that they were collected and guarded, just as the colors of various wavelengths coalesce in the sun's light."

This gave birth to a desire to share with others "the beauty of remembering him as a son, a friend, and a witness to a 'simple' life — that is, a life that is neither disconnected nor jaded, and therefore focused and at peace. Carlo taught us that finding this interior unity is paramount. He received this gift from God and decided not to hide it out of convenience or embarrassment. His instinct was to point out that the individual events coming together in our lives are not interrelated like pebbles on the seashore, but are rather interconnected in the great mystery called 'the glory of God.'"

Monsignor also notes in his testimony that life does not occur by chance or blind fate, but is rather "a gift" through which "God makes his presence felt in the mundane." Such a worldview is almost miraculous in an adolescent, but not impossible. Carlo was a visible confirmation of this. Such a worldview is capable of implanting an unsuspected meaning in our daily lives; a depth and a light that may not be noticeable on the surface, but does constitute the foundation of things. Whoever has faith sees things more deeply and sees them far in advance. We might think that such reflections are easy for us when things are going well, when we are healthy and fortunate, when we are happy with our lives. But what if things turn upside down? What if our plans don't come to fruition, if we are sick, or if something unexpectedly upends us and we see nothing ahead but darkness? Can we still say, "We have seen his glory"? Wouldn't it then be saying something derisive? Indeed, it would be if we had a very vague conception of God — like many — as simply someone who fulfills our desires, someone who plugs holes whenever there's a leak, someone whom we hold responsible for everything and accuse when things don't go well, as if he were simply supposed to take our view of everything. But this is not the Christian God, according to Monsignor Poma, "it is not the God who lies in the manger at Christmas, the God who hangs upon the cross on Good Friday. The God that human beings put their faith in can take many forms. The God of the Christian Faith is present in even our most disastrous situations by going to the extreme of death. Even human impotence can be a locus of divine glory. Carlo's young age, his organized way of heading into the future, the vicious illness that took his life; all of this became a singular, incredibly efficacious grace for the entire community and beyond. Carlo himself became a grace for us, and today it is even clearer that we can feel him as a shining friend of God's glory."

Carlo understood well that only through humility and

docility to the Spirit could he reach the complete communion with the Trinity he longed for. Monsignor Poma writes: "Even the world in which we live (in which Carlo lived with a rich vivaciousness for fifteen years) should not find it very hard to see itself in the enlightening words that Saint Paul wrote to his friend and collaborator: 'For men will be lovers, lovers of money, proud, arrogant, abusive, disobedient to their parents, ungrateful, unholy ... swollen with conceit, lovers of pleasure rather than lovers of God, holding the form of religion but denying the power of it' (2 Tm 3:2-5). This is the way of the world in every age, and there is plenty of evidence for it. In all this, how happy and fortunate are those who know 'how precious is your love, O God!' and who experience that precisely in this situation they have the opportunity to give witness to the Lord and receive from him 'wisdom for salvation through faith in Christ Jesus' so that not even your enemies can resist or overcome it. Carlo experienced the very foundation of that promise."

Monsignor Poma also writes that, unfortunately, "we tend to think that because a Christian lives with a clean, attentive, friendly soul that he should always be welcomed, understood, and recognized with affection and respect. But this is not always the case! I can't tell you how many times Carlo's counter-culturalism lead to serious trials. He often felt alone and was an object of derision. He never really talked to me about this suffering, and he never complained about it. We know how easily a talented and likable boy who is polite and intelligent, and who guards himself against coarseness and boastfulness, is looked down upon or made the butt of jokes by people who hide behind a wall of insolence and cockiness. But fortunately, Carlo never had it in him to present himself as superior or as a model adolescent. He was easygoing, not naïve, and he never had a superiority complex even though he was endowed with many talents. He knew how to be friendly, humble, and attentive to the value of his choices." Monsignor Poma also adds a personal note: "Many who knew Carlo agree that it was enough that he simply show 'how he felt on the inside' with no desire to fool people. Whenever he would confide something in me, I came away with this conviction: because he was such a straight shooter, he knew how to handle anything life handed him. He knew how to smile with frankness, to understand the souls of others, and to refrain from inappropriately judging them. The 'Christian' imprint on his soul was so deep that he would willingly give the benefit of the doubt whenever there were differences of opinion or whenever there were hints of presumptuousness on the part of his dialogue partner. This is where the grace of his good nature and level-headedness was most evident. It was as if the most difficult differences were precisely what strengthened his efforts to understand the other person, to serve as a mediator, and to engage in good humor. Truly 'his religion was not simply an appearance.' He thrived on that 'interior force' that gave him strength."

Monsignor Poma recalled Carlo's impressive confidence. This teenager relied on "the strength of those intuitions that come about as a miracle of grace. We were once talking about repetitiousness of prayers and the struggle to keep prayer fresh. This led Carlo to make this assertion: "Father, tell me if I'm wrong, but the Lord is the only person that we don't have to ask if he's available. I can always confide something in him. I can also complain or question him in silent moments and tell him the things that I don't understand. Then I find within me some word he sends me; some passage from the Gospel that cloaks me in security and confidence.'"

There is no doubt that Carlo showed a deep interest in

Sacred Scripture from a young age. He was fascinated by the life of Jesus, Our Lady, and the saints. Often, when passing in front of a church, he would ask permission to enter so that he could greet Jesus and "blow him a kiss." Whenever his parents gave him a little money, he loved to buy a rose and leave it as an offering to Mary. Whenever he was on a nature walk with his parents and his dogs, he loved to collect wild flowers and make a bouquet for the Virgin Mary. His family never tried to block these habits. In his bedroom he kept a portrait of the Merciful Jesus and a figure of the Infant of Prague. He was consecrated to the latter during a pilgrimage to Arenzano where there was a shrine to the Infant.

He considered it a special grace to make his first Communion at the age of seven in the monastery of the sisters of the Immaculate Conception of the Virgin Mary in Perego. From that point on, he never missed a daily appointment for Mass and the recitation of the Rosary. Every day, he loved to read a page of the Gospels or some other biblical passage. Even before he ever had time to study theological concepts, he put them into practice in his way of living. He was precocious in experiencing the things that the great spiritual masters explained to their disciples. But he did it in a natural, almost spontaneous way with no academic pretense and without arcane explanation. He tasted the sweetness of meeting Jesus from an early age.

When at the age of fifteen he was confronted with his illness, he was already mature enough spiritually to accept it with Jesus' help. Anyone who came into contact with him could sense this interior richness welling up from his heart making him a living witness to the Risen Christ. One look at his face was enough to see that he had discovered that higher dimension that everyone is called to. His smile communicated something from beyond — it radiated divine grace.

His face never failed to fill others with serenity, leading them to reflect on their own way of living. No one could remain indifferent in his presence!

His parents, too, were often stunned by the fascination that their son provoked in the people who met him. Everyone perceived some touch of the divine. They marveled at the depth of his interior life. His pastor explains that Carlo was an "absolutely normal" kid, "but with an absolutely unique spiritual harmony. ... He never appeared formal even though he was gifted with an attentive, pleasant, and energetic personality. He had a surprising ability to pose questions that really mattered. ... He never gave the impression of being a 'routine' Christian. Carlo left us at a moment in life when one looks to the future with optimism ... while at the same time giving us a taste of something that was even more fascinating: his simplicity." In fact, there is no doubt that "a simple person is a not an empty or inconsiderate person. Simplicity is, in fact, the opposite of duplicitous and is therefore synonymous with straightforwardness and guilelessness. It was so easy to approach him at any time. ... I could perceive in Carlo the makings of an absolutely normal life, but one that was extraordinarily harmonious. There was nothing ostentatious, no desire to appear 'special,' no desire on his part to give the impression of being superior. To the contrary, he always appeared at ease in letting his true self be seen, his zest for life and many interests, his simple style and straightforward way of speaking (in the sense that he was never two-faced or manipulative). And he was indeed a gifted kid, as anyone could tell you: He was highly intelligent, practical, and responsible. He had a good sense of humor and a clear view of what his uncompromising values were. He was candid and affectionate, but without pride and possessiveness. He was passionate about his plans and knew where to devote his talents and energy. At the same time, he was patient when it came to group projects, and feelings of resentment and stubbornness were foreign to him." Monsignor Poma stresses that Carlo had no interest in standing out from the crowd or "being divisive, even though he was always ready for a great conversation and was indeed a great conversationalist. He was sober in life and realistic in his aspirations. Anyone who knew him discovered an uncommon sense of 'pleasant fairness' that definitely had its roots in Christianity."

All this made Carlo a unique light, his pastor explains. In fact, "there is widespread agreement among those who lived, worked, and played with him about his character: his friends — both boys and girls — his parents, those who worked at the parish, and the direct knowledge that I had of him in extemporaneous exchanges about what he was up to and what his plans were, in his spiritual dialogue, always so clear and synthetic, in which he would begin with his lived experience and the questions that he would pose in his search for his Christian 'identity.' Especially when he would avail himself of the Sacrament of Reconciliation. ... Carlo was aware that his spiritual practices and expressions were 'special.' Even though he was incapable of polemics and impoliteness, he could still speak passionately about his personal experience of encountering the substance of the Gospels. It was this aspect of his personality that convinced me the most that Carlo had received an out-of-the-ordinary spiritual gift. For this reason, because of his simplicity of soul, his life could be a visible message particularly well adapted to speak to Christians — especially young people — today. He was able to speak with clear and incisive understanding of the lifestyles, choices, and challenges we face today."

Carlo is not the sole example of teenage holiness we have

in the Church's rich tradition. We can think of Maria Goretti, for example, a martyr at the tender age of twelve; or Dominic Savio, a pupil of Don Bosco, who died at fourteen. We can add Tarcisius, a martyr for saving the Eucharist, or José Sanchez Del Rio, who was martyred at fourteen-years-old while leading a service of Eucharistic adoration during the revolt of the *Cristeros*. There is also Rolando Rivi, killed out of *odium fidei* at fourteen because he was wearing a seminarian's cassock. Nor can we forget Louis Gonzaga, who converted at seven-years-old, and at eleven renounced his title of marquise; and Francesco and Jacinta Marto, the young Fatima visionaries, who died at ten-and-a-half-years-old and nine-years-old respectively. There is also Laura Vicuña, who died at twelve-years-old after having been beaten by her mother's lover, and Antonietta Meo, who died when she was almost seven-years-old.

It is clear from these examples that young people can live with very strong convictions that lead them to form a close friendship with God. In many cases, adolescent holiness reaches its peak expression in martyrdom, the spilling of one's blood out of faithfulness to Christ. This is the oldest form of sanctity recognized by the Church since her earliest days. For adolescents and children, martyrdom seems almost spontaneous and immediate since they have not had the time to mature and conform themselves to a more deliberative and plodding "adult" holiness.

In addition, we cannot overlook the fact that adolescents like Carlo are able to form a close, vibrant relationship with God through a faith that is "childlike" — as the Gospels teach — rather than "childish." A case in point is Saint Thérèse of Lisieux, who made a promise at six-years-old never to deny God anything. This simple gesture became the hallmark of her entire life: to trust the Father just like any child would throw itself in the arms of a parent. Similarly, Carlo bet his entire existence on Jesus. In fact, from the time he was little — and especially since his first Communion — he hardly ever missed an occasion to participate at daily Mass and recite the Rosary, as well as to visit the Lord in Eucharistic adoration. Even engaged in this intense spiritual life, Carlo never lived in isolation. Rather, he always took the time to visit friends and to live his life with immense joy, placing his talents at the service of others.

Perhaps his most remarkable talent was in computer programming. To everyone's astonishment, he even had a knack for deciphering advanced engineering codes. As he improved his computing skills, he offered them to help friends, Jesuit volunteers, members of the parish, and his mother in designing a site that became known as the Pontificia Accademia Cultorum Martyrum.

His generosity was boundless. He paid attention to everyone. He cared about the problems of foreigners, the disabled, poor children, and beggars. He looked for the good in everyone, and even those who were far from the Lord found in him an unconscious motive to search for the Truth. In imitation of our Eucharistic Lord, Carlo's generosity toward his neighbors and his desire to pray for them was so connatural that when leukemia finally ravaged his body, he was able to offer it to God for the good of the Church and the pope.

His long hours in front of the Most Holy Sacrament taught him to see the world through God's eyes, to expand his horizons, and to exit his comfort zone and not rely on feelings of security. He was always prepared to go out toward others, especially those who were far away. As Pope Francis is fond of saying, he liked "to go out to the most marginalized" to transmit the message of a Church always looking outward and never bent inwardly on herself.

His most famous quote was: "The Eucharist is my highway to heaven!" These words express his entire life program, his passion for God and for the human person, his aspirations for the things of heaven, where every tear will be wiped away. These words also express his boundless love for Christ and his creatures, a cry of hope for a better future, and a confirmation that faith is the upward force that allows us to see beyond the horizon of this world.

According to Monsignor Poma: "Carlo really perceived the potential and value of his life. He understood that it was a total gift that had been placed into his hands: He instinctively perceived its gratuitousness and his responsibility to make it bear fruit, and he was happy to make it do so. This was the core Eucharistic aspect of his life: To perceive it as a 'blessing' and a gift; something to be shared for the glory of God. This was the root of his attraction to Communion in the Eucharist: with his body having been given, and his blood having been poured out ... the little things that vie for young people's attention end up being such a disappointment; but when the Lord knocks on the door, we know he is ready to give us a taste of the harmony of the goodness of the world to come. I can simply tell you that Carlo believed this without hesitation, and he began the journey of faith, a remarkably fruitful endeavor for any young person. He didn't regard life as a sort of idealized 'illusion.' He loved it as it really was. He 'listened' to it grow from the waters of the Eucharist: a sacrament so dear to him."

Carlo saw in the Eucharist God's greatest expression of love. It represents God's bending to humanity, his compassion, his full participation in the human condition except for sin, and his mercy. For Carlo, the Eucharist was the best way to thank God for his benefits. It was an assurance of his communion with us and a privileged opportunity to adore the

Lord in the flesh. The moments of silence that Carlo spent in the presence of the Most Holy Sacrament were the cornerstone of his life. They gave him the opportunity to retrace his entire existence back to its source. It was the high point of his daily life, a chance to taste God, the love of his life, and to speak intimately with him. Just as a husband takes the time to admire his wife, so Carlo silently adored Jesus and praised him for his gifts.

In the Eucharistic mystery, Carlo developed his affective maturity toward Christ. This became the principal characteristic of his spirituality. Bathing in the light of the Eucharist was his way of entering the mystery of God's heart. He found strength to confront his daily work, to grow in friendship with him, and to feel and think what Jesus would do in his place. It was a key moment of conforming his existence to God's. In this encounter of hearts and in Carlo's innocence, he developed the capacity to love with the same Divine Heart — that is, without measure, giving himself entirely in charitable service to all those around him.

His certainty that the Eucharist has the power to transform hearts led him often to say: "The more often we receive the Eucharist, the more we become like Jesus and the more we get a foretaste of heaven." The ability to imitate the Master is indeed one of the principal fruits of participating in Communion with his Body and Blood. Carlo understood this from a very young age, and it became a principal part of his daily life. The closer we draw to the Eucharist, the more we are transformed by it, because the presence of Christ transforms the "old man" into the "new man," and the latter can set the world on fire with the flame of charity.

Carlo's way of living gave flesh to the words of the martyr Saint Ignatius of Antioch, who in a letter to the Philadelphians called the Eucharist "the medicine for immortality and the antidote against death so that we may always live with Jesus Christ." Carlo perceived from an early age that without the help of divine grace we can do nothing. God's power completely overpowers man's impotence, and with that strength, man can accomplish extraordinary things. Carlo demonstrated that he was clearly aware of this when he said, "Without Him we can do nothing." It was an attestation of his faith and complete abandonment to God's providence. It was his confession of willingness to be an instrument of salvation in his hands, thus becoming the means by which Christ could bring his love and consolation to those most in need. Carlo understood that he had to take care of the Body of Christ in everyone he met throughout the day: the poor, the sick, the elderly, the disabled, immigrants, and sinners. He recognized in everyone the face of Jesus marred by evil, sickness, sin, and human injustice. But underneath, he saw the inestimable worth of human dignity.

When Saint Catherine of Siena asked Jesus to give her the power to love all men, he responded by telling her of the ineffable beauty of the human soul. In the same way, Carlo found the power to exercise charity toward those most in need and to help his brothers and sisters in an attitude of perpetual adoration of the Most Holy Sacrament. His Eucharistic devotion inspired him to save his money to help the poor, the elderly, the cloistered nuns, priests, and foreigners. He had no doubt that charity had the power to transform everything, but most of all it was the key to unlock the treasures of Paradise. All of this was possible because of the union he found with Christ in daily Communion, the apex of his day. Through the Eucharist, he said, "you go directly to heaven, and we are given the opportunity to do it everyday."

In the school of Jesus, we learn to give of ourselves a

little more each day. We learn to live the fullness of charity from its very source. Knowing that we have to make sacrifices and learn perseverance to love, Carlo once said: "Life is a gift, because as long as we are on this planet, we can grow in our ability to love. The more we learn to love, the more we will enjoy eternal blessedness with God." For Carlo, "every minute that passes in vain is a missed opportunity to become more holy." Time, therefore, is too precious to waste in things "displeasing to God." Carlo used to say that the Lord created time for us, and that through his Son, Jesus, God has taught us to live every moment of time in communion with him. In Jesus, the gap between the eternal and the temporal is bridged, and we thus have the opportunity to live in a special time (*kairos*) in communion with the Most Holy Trinity in God's everlasting "today." It was the sacraments, and especially the Eucharist, that for Carlo were the living sign of God's presence among us.

This certainty of his was based on the fact that our existence is simply an opportunity to accept the love Christ offers us, and to respond to it positively. To accept God's love in our lives means to love our "brothers and sisters" who reflect the face of the Savior by using the supernatural means God has given us in the sacraments. It means making the attempt to change our mind-set and take on that of the Gospel, to opt for self-giving rather than self-centeredness, to live in simplicity rather than arrogance and pride. It means to not take advantage of the other, to listen to him, to help him, and to make the effort to understand his ideas. It means not imposing our will, but opening ourselves in dialogue; not disregarding others or considering anyone a waste of humanity. Christ spent his life to restore man's dignity, so our job is to recognize that dignity in every human person we meet.

Carlo understood that we always run the risk of going

astray and abandoning the way Christ has shown us, forgetting him and living as if he didn't exist. Carlo could see many examples of those who lost their way and spent their days far from the Lord. This is why he often said, "Everybody is born unique, but many die as photocopies." He was saddened by the number of people he saw abandoning a coherent life of faith either because of inconvenience or boredom, and thus throwing away the compass that would orient their lives.

In a homily given in memory of Carlo, his pastor said: "We all know either directly or indirectly where misplaced goals lead us in life; how they eventually show themselves as useless or half hearted attempts to marginalize things that frighten us. ... Where will we anchor our heart if we lose sight of the presence of the Lord within us? But we indeed know the gift of the Father in heaven and we have hope in the Son who invites us to follow in his footsteps. Therefore, through vigilance and prayer, we can reach that lucid, serene, reassuring sobriety that distinguishes the Christian life. The morning sets the tone of the entire day. The Gospel gives us a wonderful suggestion this evening: 'During the day, Jesus was teaching in the temple area, but at night he would leave and stay at the place called the Mount of Olives. And all the people would get up early each morning to listen to him in the temple area.' The morning is a graced time to listen to him. For kids and teens, how important that morning time is to listen and discover what is deep inside them! It has only been a few years since Carlo's death, and with time his special characteristics have become clearer to me. He had acquired this evangelical way of balancing family life, school, friendships, and an outlook that was free of anxiety, living in the present without hastiness and listlessness."

Monsignor Poma continues his testimony with some specific examples: "I am convinced that Carlo had the grace to cultivate a state of soul rare for his age: the certainty that the Lord inspires and guards our good intentions in this life. This state of soul gave Carlo the power to confront different times and circumstances throughout this life. A clear sign of this was the following: He always found time for the Lord, and he did so even where there were pleasant and interesting alternatives for him to choose. Perhaps this evening, thanks to our fond memories of Carlo, we are encouraged to rediscover the beauty and essence of Christian freedom: A Christian knows with good reason that he is not the absolute, autonomous center of deciding what is good and what is bad for himself and others. The Lord, the source of all life, knows better than me, and he communicates what it is that makes my life good. In communion with the Lord, I can thank him for this sensibility: I didn't create it, it was rather given to me. For this reason, I seek to form my life thanks to that primordial gift by which the Lord allows me to see my worth. Carlo was happy spending time in the Lord's presence. After some time in adoration, he would get up and take with him whatever the Lord was asking of him. It is a great gift to be able to live in lucid, serene sobriety. It is an extraordinary gift when a young boy perceives this from the earliest stages of his life."

There are so many dramas and disappointments that can dull the soul and make it unresponsive to Christ's call to charity and to open ourselves to others. Carlo used to say that it was enough to not be too concerned with yourself, but rather to turn your attention to the needs of your brothers and sisters. He would often say, "Sadness is simply a look of self-pity directed at yourself, and happiness is to turn our gaze to God." Only in Christ can man find true happiness, something that no person can take away or dilute. Happiness is what everyone aims for but few find, because they get lost in thousands of mundane concerns that distract their gaze from heaven. But Carlo teaches us that true happiness consists not only in finding ways to divert our attention away from ourselves, but to put God in first place, and consequently also our brothers and sisters. "Our ultimate goal must be the Infinite and not the finite," he used to say. He would add: "If God possesses our hearts, then we will possess the Infinite."

Unfortunately, a lot of people are pulled into the world and its empty promises. There are those who have the ability to judge what is really right and good, but the majority prefer to conform their behavior to whatever is temporary and fleeting. Carlo used to say, "Find God and you will find the meaning of your life." He could never understand "why many people are so concerned with the beauty of their bodies rather than spending time on the beauty of their souls."

Carlo had the gift of perceiving a dimension of reality that infinitely transcends the finite world. He considered the soul to be inserted in a plan of salvation that does not end with death, but rather is a preparation to confront death as a necessary step to the next stage. Carlo lived his life constantly in the Lord's presence. He invited others to beware of the risk of becoming too attached to the present moment, to fleeting fashions, to futile pursuits, thus ruining the ability to look beyond and to raise one's head to notice the transcendent dimension. He would say, "Conversion is nothing other than turning one's gaze away from the inferior to the superior. It takes nothing more than diverting our eyes to another direction." It takes nothing more than a change of focus and an act of re-concentrating your vision on a horizon that goes beyond the limits of this visible world. This certainly requires sacrifice and strength, but it leads to an abiding happiness that nothing can take away. Carlo invites us to choose Christ and to shun the allurements of this world, because he was convinced that at the end of our lives we will be judged by the love we should have had for God and for our brothers and sisters rather than on the "vain successes" and "ephemeral powers" that many are ambitious for, and for which people are willing to risk their eternal soul. This was attested to by Jacinta, the visionary at Fatima: "If men knew what eternity was, they would change their lives completely." This is why it is necessary to place God at the center of our existence, to change gears, to cross the Red Sea and find the joy and strength of the Resurrection. Carlo used to say, "We must make our Exodus from sin with complete conviction," knowing that the things that appear so attractive and unrenounceable now will one day be revealed for what they truly are: utterly false.

Carlo invites us to count the days we have on this earth and to consider that, even if they happen to be many, life is brief in comparison with eternity. Therefore, it was inconceivable for him that anyone could fail to meditate on his own destiny and waste his existence by not using his God-given talents to bear fruit. Carlo would say, "What good would it be for a human being to win a thousand battles if he is incapable of conquering his very self?"

Communion with Christ leads to being coheirs of his riches and citizens of his heavenly paradise. For Carlo, any act of self-renunciation on this earth has a corresponding and immeasurable grace in heaven. We simply have to choose between everlasting happiness and resigning ourselves to a measly satisfaction with this passing world. This is the message Carlo wanted to share with everyone he met. To achieve this Christian happiness, it does no good to give in to the prevailing mind-set. We must be countercultural and give our hearts to God who alone offers us true peace. Giving our hearts means performing an act of faith and opening our hearts just as Mary did in her "fiat" to God through the Archangel Gabriel. This is the way we show ourselves ready to do God's divine will no matter the cost, because only in that way can we be sure we will reach our destiny as his creatures.

The most important thing, in fact, is "not love itself, but the glory of God." Everything else will pass away. Stubborn attachment to our will does no good, because our will alone is not a reliable compass. The only true compass is God's will, who alone knows what we need to orient ourselves and to reach the ultimate goal of heaven. To work for the glory of God as Carlo did means to make the fundamental choice to follow Christ, to acknowledge his presence in our lives, to put him in first place, and to bring him to others so that they, too, can participate in his riches. This requires humility, something that Carlo cultivated at the young age of fifteen as he spent his final days lying in a hospital bed, from which he would often say serenely: "I am dying peacefully because I have lived my life without wasting a single minute of it in things that displease God."

How we wish we could say the same thing in our final moments! And to think that this wisdom proceeded from the mouth of a fifteen-year-old! How we all should content ourselves with closing our eyes in the moment of death only to wake up in God's arms! How we all should look forward to falling asleep in the Lord as the just reward for having touched upon that intense love that requires us to follow Christ! To have achieved such a level of spiritual maturity in so few years brings to mind a passage from the Book of Wisdom: "In the eyes of the foolish they seemed to have died, and their departure was thought to be an affliction, and their going from us to be their destruction; but they are at peace. For though in the sight of men they were punished, their hope is full of immortality. Having been disciplined a little, they will receive great good, because God tested them and found them worthy of himself; like gold in the furnace he tried them, and like a sacrificial burnt offering he accepted them." (Wis 3:2–6).

Carlo had to endure many trials, but he never turned his gaze in upon himself. He was always ready to reach out to others; to come out of himself and to prefer God's will over his own. He had a natural and serene detachment from earthly things because he knew that he was ultimately going to meet Christ, the Lord with whom he had formed such an intimate friendship.

First of all, I would like to thank Monsignor Dario Edoardo Viganò, Prefect of the Secretariat for Communications at the Holy See, who kindly wrote the preface for this biography. I would also like to thank Monsignor Gianfranco Poma, pastor of the parish of *Santa Maria Segreta* in Milan and Mother Anna Maria Canopi for their contributions.

I am also most grateful to Carlo's parents who experienced first-hand the marvelous graces that God performed in their son's life, because he can complete them in any young life. I am equally thankful to everyone who has helped spread the message of this amazing teenager whose fame has spread throughout the world.

THE FIRST STEPS

Carlo Acutis was born on May 3, 1991, in London, a city his parents, Andrea and Antonia, moved to for purposes of work. Witnessing the birth of their first son was a most joyful day for this Christian family. The baby was baptized the following May 18 in the church of Our Lady of Dolours in London, taking the name "Carlo Maria Antonio." His uncle Carlo and his maternal aunt Luana served as godparents. Years later, Carlo would acknowledge the importance of this sacrament that inserted him into the bosom of the Church, because it "opens the door of salvation to a soul as it revests it with divine life. Anyone who doesn't recognize the infinite value of this sacrament aside from the decorations, the cake, and the white dress has no idea of the meaning of this great gift that God has given to mankind."

Carlo lived a peaceful life in London with his mother, who, with the help of a babysitter, took care of him. Their stay in the British capital lasted until September 1991 when the family remigrated to Italy. His parents enrolled him in an elementary school in Milan when he was four years old. He was happy to attend because, being an only child, it gave him the chance to get to know other kids. Carlo had a pleasant and peaceful personality. He never reacted violently, even when others would pick on him. One Polish child of a very different temperament grew angry with him because he wanted Carlo to take revenge on friends who poked fun at him. But Carlo never did. Whenever kids told him to retaliate, Carlo would respond, "The Lord would not be pleased if I reacted violently." Otherwise, he had a likable personality and was readily accepted by other kids.

His appealing personality and his easy going manner made it easy for him to dialogue with others. It was virtually impossible not to like Carlo, who was both spontaneous and laid-back. His good humor even won over those who could hardly stand kids. A girl his age had this to say: "I always remember Carlo as having an angelic quality. He had deep faith in God and a purity that you could perceive whenever you were in his presence. One of his greatest virtues was his humility. He was generous with other kids. I remember that whenever other kids would threaten him in some way, he never reacted violently. We would get mad at him because we thought he should threaten them back, but there was no way of convincing him." Whoever had the chance to know him — parents, friends, acquaintances — all considered him to be a lively, good-natured child who was well liked, but also reflective, preferring to be alone sometimes.

Throughout his childhood, he spent summers — from June to September — with his maternal grandparents in Centola, a village in the province of Salerno located in the hills above Lake Palinuro. That was the place his great-grandparents met. His great-grandmother was a lovely and highly respected woman, because as a rich landowner she was very generous to anyone in need. Vacation time was an opportunity for Carlo to immerse himself in the incredible natural beauty of the area. He spent much of his time by the sea. He had time not only to rest but also to have fun and to form new friendships. In such a healthy and rustic environment, Carlo adopted many of the attractive qualities of the locals, including spontaneity and an openness toward others.

The villagers of Centola admired this well-behaved, simple, lively kid who came to spend the summer months with them in the country. They saw him participate at Mass each evening after returning from the beach, and this only increased their admiration. The farmers in the area always considered him one of their own, and they happily offered him gifts of fruit and fresh eggs. His openness allowed him to make many friends. The time Carlo spent in Centola remained one of his fondest memories and filled him with a zeal for life.

To help with babysitting, Carlo's grandparents were fortunate to find a Polish student who helped care for him for almost four years. She treated him like a son. Here is how she described their relationship: "When I first set eyes on Carlo, I was shocked at how much he looked like one of those 'little angels' you see in famous Italian paintings. His eyes radiated a light that seemed to come from deep within. His spirituality was certainly saintly because it is hard to find a kid his age who goes to Mass and prays the rosary every day! When he was about five-years-old, his mother and I took him on a little pilgrimage to the Shrine of Pompei. We could clearly see the deep devotion he had for Our Lady. He even made a special consecration of himself to Our Lady of the Rosary in

Pompei, after which we joined him in praying the Rosary in front of the miraculous image of the Holy Virgin."

After summer break in 1997, Carlo, then six, enrolled in the Istituto San Carlo di Milano, a prestigious and well-known private school. Because his mother wanted him to attend a school closer to home, she transferred him to the Istituto Tommaseo delle suore Marcelline after only three months. At first, he wasn't happy to leave his friends and teacher at *San Carlo,* but he soon made new friends and settled into his new school. He instantly felt comfortable with the Marcelline sisters, and they in turn were happy to have him. His cheerfulness, respect, love for life, and sense of obedience made him "special" in the eyes of several sisters. They admired his punctuality, sense of duty, diligence, good manners, and the affection he showed for others immediately upon meeting them. For his part, Carlo made a lot of friends who gravitated toward him during playtime.

One of his elementary school schoolmates recalls his ingratiating smile, his rambunctious joy, his big-heartedness, and his selfless willingness to help. His generosity and high ideals were well known, as he was always ready to defend anyone who was the brunt of mean jokes. He was also known to willingly help anyone having difficulty with schoolwork.

There was one particular personality trait in Carlo that virtually everyone agrees on. Whenever he was on his bicycle headed for school or to play with friends, he always stopped to talk to the building custodians. The majority of these custodians were immigrants, but that didn't make any difference to Carlo. He was friendly and cordial with everyone no matter who they were. It made no difference what race, language, or religion they were. He always looked straight to the heart, and in everyone he found a unique person worth discovering. The custodians he formed relationships with marveled that a kid from such a well-to-do family would want to spend time talking with them. But this was entirely natural for Carlo since he considered everyone a brother or sister in Christ.

On June 16, 1998, the Wednesday after the Solemnity of the Body and Blood of Christ, in the church of the monastery of the Romite nuns in Perego, he received his first Communion. This was a fundamental step in the spiritual development of a boy who wanted to live life to the fullest and get to know Jesus even better.

SCHOOL

When Carlo successfully completed elementary school, he moved up to middle school at the Istituto Tommaseo delle suore Marcelline, where he studied from September 2002 to September 2005. It must be said that he was not among the first in his class, but there were certain subjects — such as computing — in which he excelled. He had special and extraordinary gifts that allowed him to learn many things quickly and without the help of his teachers or adults. His mother was always impressed that her son learned how to play the saxophone — a particularly difficult instrument to learn at his age — entirely on his own.

Since his mother was often away at work in Milan, she wanted to find an assistant to help him with his homework. She was fortunate to find a qualified young lady. A special relationship formed between her and Carlo. Carlo trusted her very much and confided in her, seeking her advice in many things. Years later, this young lady would recount how Carlo was always ready to help his schoolmates when they were having trouble with their schoolwork. She considered this a special sign of Carlo's generosity and charity towards others. He was also most considerate of the religious sisters and his teachers. In particular, she recalls how during the Christmas fair Carlo always used his savings to buy gifts for everyone, even the teachers.

This au pair considered Carlo a balanced, good-mannered, prudent boy who was mature beyond his years. His nobility of soul, discretion, and humility prevented him from ever showing any superiority over other children. Unlike his peers, he never bragged about his family's house, money, cars, and he never cared much about the latest fashion. Carlo was most remarkable for never conforming to the prevailing mind-set. His *au pair* was quite struck with these traits. He even managed to convince her to go with him to daily Mass.

Her testimony is quite striking: "I will never forget how special he was. He was so different from others. So good. I am convinced that Carlo had an extraordinary relationship with the Lord. He always kept a beautiful image of Our Lord in the place where we would study. Woe to anyone who moved it! I must say that it is very difficult to find boys like this, especially in today's world."

Carlo's teachers agree that Carlo was a peaceable and well-behaved boy with a great sense of discipline, eschewing the misbehavior of most of his peers. He never engaged in the things that got the other children in trouble. One of his teachers called him "a true gentleman," adding that he was always generous and ready to help those in need. Shy by nature, he avoided flattery and compliments and was widely sought out by his classmates. He often intervened if arguments between his classmates got heated. His concern for the forgotten and the marginalized was well known. He was particularly helpful to one boy who had trouble learning and making friends.

His sympathetic and caring personality rubbed off on others. Upbeat and at ease, he enjoyed telling funny stories. He loved to make short amateur films and show them to his friends. He always gave his best effort at everything he did. He threw himself into cooking because he wanted to become a first-class chef like the one his grandparents had in Turin. He never settled for mediocrity, but always strove to do his best. The chef marveled at the boy's ambition and was impressed that Carlo was so interested in knowing his recipes. The chef immediately noted the interest, refined manners, and good behavior of the boy, who never failed to rush into the kitchen and thank him for such a delicious meal.

Carlo showed the same behavior toward his classmates, who were always amazed at his friendship and kindness. As is often the case, some of his peers did not understand Carlo's habits, such as his aversion to taking advantage of his social status by traveling to exotic places and having all the latest electronic gear and hi-fi stereo equipment. Some considered him too spiritual and intellectual for his age. In particular, they couldn't understand why Carlo wanted to go to Assisi for vacation when he had the economic means for much more fascinating destinations. There were those who considered him a "victim of his parents" since they always took him to Assisi. But we know from the personal testimony of his spiritual advisor that Carlo felt he could never visit Assisi enough because he felt happier there than anywhere else.

In fact, he spent the greater part of his vacations at a family house in Assisi. He enjoyed taking walks in the woods with his parents and dogs. A lot of times, he simply liked to play with little kids, such as Mattia and Jacopo, whom he got to know through their grandmother Mirella. He loved to run in the open fields with his friends and go for hikes in the country. He often brought his camera on these excursions so that he could take photos of himself with his friends. He also loved to visit the local swimming club where he made friends with the workers who cleaned the pool. One of those workers was struck by Carlo's sweet disposition toward animals, such as the little insects he would save from drowning in the pool. In the summer of 2006, he asked his parents whether they would let him get a job serving food and drinks at the swimming pool since he wanted to prove he could hold a job and earn money to help the poor.

His behavior not only attracted the attention of his peers, but adults too. Sometimes he would work for hours designing computer programs, making calculations, or solving mathematical problems that no one else could understand, and he did it all to help his friends. His talent was admired by many friends who considered him a mathematical and computer genius. Whenever someone asked, he would teach them programming skills or simply the basics of using a personal computer. He was convinced that everyone needs to know how to use a computer well; otherwise, we become isolated from the world and unhirable in the workplace.

Carlo was also known for holding firm convictions. He was repulsed by passing fads, commercialism, and consumerism. He was very counter-cultural in this regard, but he didn't care much about what people thought of him. He used to say that what is most lacking in today's world is a "critical spirit." We are easily misled by whatever the media tells us and forget to think for ourselves. Carlo used to dress in a simple, non-fashionable way and was often made fun of by those showing off the latest styles. Carlo was also critical of television. He liked quiz shows, action films — especially police movies — but he closed his eyes whenever programs or advertisements with explicit sexual references came on. He couldn't stand vulgarity and immodesty. It is interesting to note that, after his death, a scan of his personal computer revealed that he had only visited sites dedicated to holy shrines, the lives of the saints, the Bible, and the Virgin Mary. He eschewed vain and dangerous searches that so many young people fall into.

His candor was noted by more than his parents. Rajesh, a domestic helper at his house, also noted it. Carlo was not one to be embarrassed by certain actions. He was spontaneous and free-spirited. His relationship with girls was also friendly, full of respect, and affectionate. His family used to joke that he had a lot of sweethearts, but for him they were simply good friends.

Carlo formed a particularly close friendship with one girl because of her interest in computer programming. She asked him to give her some lessons. This girl once asked him to give her a "little kiss" because she was sad. Her boyfriend had just broken up with her. Carlo gave her a little kiss on the cheek to cheer her up a bit. This was the only "little kiss" in his lifetime. Carlo used to say that "the body is the temple of the Holy Spirit," and it had to be respected according to God's commandments without rushing into things as many teenagers do today who are overwhelmed by social pressures and bombarded with false messages, especially given the spread of pornography. Carlo often reprimanded friends whenever he noticed them falling into harmful relationships where young people would take advantage of one another as "objects of pleasure." It really hurt him to see so many friends "sink too deeply," and he therefore prayed that the

Lord would enlighten them with his grace.

Carlo also cultivated friendships outside school. He often met his friends to go out for a snack or to chat or play soccer in the public square in front of the Istituto Tommaseo. In all things — play, study, work — he strove to serve Jesus. He never doubted the importance of giving his entire self to Christ. Every attitude, action, and word he uttered day in and day out was always chosen in light of what pleased the Lord. He never let words of hate, derision, or insult escape his lips. His way of life reflected the Gospel values in which he believed. He never let his relationships undermine his moral integrity.

His peers took notice of his intense spiritual life. They saw him attend daily Mass with a faith that seemed to rub off on everyone else. One time, his teacher, forgetting where a specific Gospel passage was, asked him for the reference because she knew he could find it quickly. He was never afraid to talk about controversial and sensitive topics such as divorce and the Sacrament of Marriage. He was never embarrassed to affirm the Church's teaching in these areas, and he was always keen on understanding the Church's thinking on why it is important to live chastely and modestly before marriage. Whenever friends went through the drama of a parental separation, Carlo would try to console and encourage them, inviting them to his house to cheer them up. And how saddened he was by the number of acquaintances who had to endure the pain of separation and divorce!

There are countless testimonies to Carlo's extraordinary character, his intelligence, and his ability to grasp difficult concepts quickly. In particular, many testify to his humility and adherence to the Church's Magisterium on the dignity of life and other key teachings. He was well known for defending the weak and helping the neediest. There was a girl in his middle-school class who was having lots of trouble with her schoolwork. He took it upon himself to help her in the areas she found most difficult. Carlo's willingness to help and his eagerness to be a good friend even extended to little kids whom he gladly assisted with homework. During recess, he loved to go play soccer with kids from less privileged households.

Carlo's father testifies to his son's enormous patience with little kids, with whom he loved to spend time. His room was full of toys that he loved to lend out to little kids, with no expectation of ever getting them back.

HIGH SCHOOL

When he turned fourteen, Carlo enrolled at the Istituto Leone XIII, a *liceo classico** run by the Jesuits in Milan. This was the perfect place for Carlo to develop further his human and Christian virtues. In particular, he was able to deepen his knowledge of the subject that fascinated him most: computer science. He joined forces with an engineering student to develop the website of the parish church of Santa Maria Segreta in Milan. Even though his studies required a lot of time, he also wanted to volunteer, teaching the *Catechism* to children preparing for Confirmation. He loved this work. The work was entirely voluntary, and when he was not able to go because of schoolwork, it pained him. It was in that year that he began to design a new internet site for the volunteers at the Istituto Leone XIII. He also

---

* A *liceo classico* is a high school whose curriculum concentrates in the humanities. It is broadly distinguished from a *liceo scientifico* which offers more technical training.

coordinated efforts to create a recruiting advertisement for Jesuit volunteers in a national contest. Still full of energy, he continued to work on the website for the Jesuit volunteers throughout the summer of 2006.

He thus proved himself a driving force not only in personal initiatives, but also in school projects. Father Roberto Gazzaniga, a Jesuit priest, testifies to Carlo's active involvement in the pastoral care of students at the Istituto Leone XIII: "Carlo enrolled at the Istituto Leone XIII, a school directed by the Society of Jesus, in the academic year of 2005–2006, choosing to attend the *liceo classico*. A student in the 4B class, he quickly — though humbly — proved that he had extraordinary human qualities." Father Gazzaniga says that, from the beginning Carlo acted as if he were already familiar with the school for some time, acting with a cordiality, familiarity, friendliness, amiability, and facility uncommon to new students. He found himself at home at the Istituto. Classmates, teachers, and staff at the school turned to him often as they were attracted by his combination of noble mannerisms and remarkable spontaneity and freshness. Carlo was enthusiastic to get heavily involved at the school, ready for new challenges and eager to make new friends. The Jesuit father also remembers how Carlo was sensitive to kids who didn't fit in so easily. From his very first day, Carlo was courageous and respectful in looking out for those who were having a hard time adjusting to the new school. Father Gazzaniga noticed Carlo's care for these classmates immediately. He remembers how Carlo used to roam the halls of the two floors of the school during the long morning break, looking to meet new friends among the kids and teachers. He would often spend a few minutes with a boy or girl who otherwise would have been alone, waiting anxiously for the break to finish. He showed an enthusiasm to get other lively and respectful kids involved with looking after the good of the school. The "old-time doorman" at the school remembers that whenever Carlo entered via another door in the morning (the so-called pool door), he would make a point to return to the main door just to say "hello" to his friend. Carlo did this routinely, distinguishing himself from kids who sometimes greeted him and sometimes didn't, depending on their mood.

Even though Carlo displayed a good nature that separated him from his peers, they never picked on him or made fun of him because of it. Carlo's well-mannered and respectful character actually won over his schoolmates when, in most cases, students would have mocked others as "goody two-shoes."

Father Gazzaniga emphasizes that Carlo always lived the faith and never hid his adherence to the Church's Magisterium, not even when he encountered opposition. One day, one of the Jesuit fathers visited Carlo's class to ask if anyone wanted to take part in an extracurricular group called the "Community of Christian Life CVX." After the priest explained the purpose of the group, Carlo was the only one who expressed interest.

His schoolmates, especially those in middle school, emphasize a few characteristics that struck them most: his cheerfulness, energy, generosity, his desire to form close friendships, and his self-discipline. They never remember him getting angry, even when provoked. They rather remember him as a boy who never shirked responsibility and whose optimism was infectious.

When Father Gazzaniga needed help in organizing the volunteer opportunities for the students, Carlo volunteered his time to develop a presentation on the various opportunities with a computer program developed by professionals called Dreamweaver. This is what kept Carlo busy through-out the summer of 2006. When the Jesuit voluntary corps were organizing summer sessions involving some parents, everyone was impressed with the liveliness of Carlo's pre-sentation, his passion, and his ingenuity in putting togeth-er a CD to stir interest among the students to get involved with volunteer work. The mothers were amazed at his orga-nization and leadership and his combination of kindness, enthusiasm, and efficiency.

Eventually, his computing skills caught the attention of a famous programmer who had written a few universi-ty textbooks. This professor was amazed that a kid his age could speak computer lingo so easily and professionally. Similarly, a noted economist and businessman noticed Carlo's extraordinary abilities in computer programming and computer science. One of his friends remembers that Carlo used to say: "If you really know how to use a com-puter, you should be able to decipher programs; otherwise, you are only a user and not a real programmer." In fact, Car-lo was able to read and understand university-level text-books on Java, C++, and Ubuntu. Many people turned to him for free lessons on programming or to prepare for ad-vanced exams in computing.

One of Carlo's friends, remembering fondly his willing-ness to help others, tells the following story. After school one day in October 2005, as they were unlocking their bikes for the ride home, a classmate of his confessed that he was terrified to receive his report card because he was expect-ing the highest marks and the other kids would make fun of him as they did in elementary and middle school. Carlo told him not to worry and that he would be there to stand up for him if he encountered any meanness from his class-mates. This shows how ready Carlo was to help introverted kids who had problems socializing.

His teachers also remember him with respect and admiration. One of his teachers remembers clearly how dedicated Carlo was to his schoolwork and his ability to collaborate with others, especially in the task of creating an advertising slogan for volunteer opportunities as the school prepared to participate in a national contest entitled, "You'll be a volunteer!"

So many kids remember him as a generous and open young man, ready to help anyone in trouble. One of his peers remembers how he stood up to defend a disabled schoolmate who was being made fun of. Carlo was never afraid to stand up to bullying, which had become so common among young people. On another occasion, Carlo came to the defense of a girl from India because she was wearing the traditional sari. Once, at his school, there was an assembly where a missionary Jesuit who had spent many years in China spoke. Carlo was horrified that his classmates chattered throughout the presentation, interfering with those who wanted to listen to the priest's fascinating experiences. In discussions and debates, Carlo was always ready to speak openly about his conviction on the dignity of human life and moral principles. Abortion was a specific issue in which Carlo staunchly defended the Church and its stance on the life of an embryo as a child of God. A high school classmate remembers an intense discussion in religion class and Carlo was the only one to voice opposition to abortion. Not long before his death, Carlo's class was given a writing assignment on how different religions addressed the issue of artificial insemination, and Carlo chose to focus on Judaism. After spending a lot of time researching the subject, he told his classmates how shocked he was to discover the sad fate of millions of frozen embryos throughout the world. He said that if he were a woman, he would perform the act of charity of adopting one of these embryos and giving that human life the possibility of living fully.

HIS LOVE FOR ANIMALS

One of Carlo's most remarkable traits was his love of animals. He especially loved cats, dogs, and goldfish. If he ever found an animal abandoned in the street, he would beg his parents to let him bring it home. He was extremely sensitive to animals and was convinced they would go to heaven after death, because he thought it was impossible for God to destine them to an eternal fate of nothingness. One of his cousins who lived in Rome tells the story that, during summer vacation in 2002, the two of them made friends with two kids from Naples, one of whom spotted a lizard lying on a rock. He killed it for no reason. Carlo was so horrified by the senseless death of the defenseless little creature that his mother had to console him for a long time, assuring him that the lizard was now happy with Jesus.

Computers were not Carlo's only passion. He was fascinated with all electronics. He used to indulge his passion by making short amateur films where animals took the leading role. He made funny movies of his dogs doing humorous things and showed them to his family and friends. His most famous were those of his "cannonball pooch" Stellina, who was a voracious eater and extremely fat, and of Briciola, his favorite dog, whom Carlo nicknamed "the seven-demoned dog," because he was a miniature Doberman and therefore very imposing. His mother had a dog named Chiara whom he nicknamed "giant rat," because she incessantly barked at everyone who trespassed on their property since she was overly protective of his mother's belongings. Some of Carlo's funniest films featured him playing the role of an evil general commanding his army of dogs as they tried to conquer the world of "monster cats" constantly at war with them. The dogs had so rehearsed their parts that they seemed true actors. Carlo would put them up against the "monster cat" Cleo, who was the supreme cat-commander trying to conquer the dog-world. He also had a dog named Poldo who starred in the role of foreign minister, and Briciola who was the supreme commander's archenemy. Everyone recognized Carlo's directing skills and his knack for making brilliant, witty films.

Besides the cats and dogs, Carlo also loved dolphins. Once on a boating excursion, he told his mother that he had asked Jesus to show him some dolphins. His prayers were answered. His grandparents also happened to be with the family that day.

Unfortunately, his maternal grandmother passed away when Carlo was only four years old. Carlo used to tell the story of how she appeared to him one day shortly after her death and asked him to pray for her because she was in purgatory. From that moment, he began to pray for her fervently and to attend Mass, for the Eucharistic Liturgy was "the most important prayer we can perform to help the departed souls to leave purgatory."

His affection for his paternal grandfather was strong despite the fact that he couldn't see him often since he lived so far away. Every time they got together, Carlo loved to sit and listen to his counsel and advice. He taught him to be extra vigilant against the vice of gluttony. Besides having long conversations with him, Carlo loved to play chess and other skill games with him. Whenever his parents took him to visit grandpa, it was like a big holiday for Carlo.

He was also very attached to both grandmothers. His paternal grandmother was half Irish and half Polish, while his maternal grandmother was all Italian. They both came from practicing Catholic families, and they were often heard saying that none of their ancestors had shown the talents Carlo had. Both grandmothers always considered Carlo a bright light of purity and generosity, and most of all, a boy of faith. Luana, his maternal grandmother, was widowed in 1995 and moved to Milan to be closer to her only daughter Antonia and her grandson. She also recalls how Carlo loved to attend daily Mass and, whenever his mother was away, how he would pout if she didn't take him to church.

THE EUCHARIST: THE HEART OF CHRIST

It is hard to grasp who Carlo really was without taking his Eucharistic spirituality into account. His daily appointment with Christ in the Eucharist was for him the center point and heart of his entire life. He firmly believed that in the Eucharist, "Jesus was really present to the world, just as when his apostles and disciples saw him walk the streets of Jerusalem." Carlo was fond of repeating a saying that reveals the depth of his Eucharist devotion: "The Eucharist is my highway to heaven!" Through his communion with the Body and Blood of Christ, Carlo would truly find a way to ascend to heaven where the Lord would be waiting for him so that he could spend eternity with him.

His mother had given him a little white stuffed lamb when he was just a baby. It was the first present he ever received, and he was very attached to it. It ended up taking on special significance in that Carlo himself was destined to be sacrificed just like the Lamb. It was a symbol of his attachment to the Immaculate Lamb, Christ the Lord, sacrificed for our salvation. Carlo was firmly convinced of the importance of Mass: "I think that many people do not fully understand the value of Mass, because if they recognized the enormous blessing we have in a Lord who gives himself as our food and drink in the Sacred Host, they would go to Mass every day to participate in the fruits of the sacrifice and let go of so many superfluous things!"

His love for the Sacrament only increased after his first Communion. With the permission of his spiritual father, he attended Mass every day. He was well aware that "souls are sanctified in an exceptional way by the fruits of daily Communion. They are strengthened especially for dangerous challenges that can jeopardize their eternal salvation." In imitation of the children in Fatima, he offered little sacrifices for those who did not love the Lord Jesus present in the Eucharist.

His spiritual father, who appreciated his deep devotion to the Eucharist and respect for priests, remembers: "Carlo was very sensitive to understanding whether priests celebrated Mass devoutly, and it saddened him to see priests rushing through the ritual. He said to me more than once that because priests 'work with the hands of Christ,' they need to witness to the Lord with enthusiasm and be lights to the world rather than machines heartlessly churning out a liturgical ritual devoid of faith." His spiritual director also recalls how Carlo spent time in Eucharistic adoration both before and after Mass "to thank Jesus for the great gift he has given man in rendering himself really present in the Sacrament of the Eucharist." More than once, "he asked how he might convince lukewarm people to attend Mass on Sunday. He said that when he spoke of the Eucharistic miracle at Lanciano and the apparition of the angel to the children of Fatima, people seemed to come alive. I encouraged him to use Scripture whenever he had the occasion to. I was very pleased by his apostolic zeal and I harbored a deep hope that Carlo might choose to be a priest someday."

Carlo was firmly convinced that the consecration was a privileged moment to ask the Lord for a specific grace. He was used to saying, "Who can intercede more for us than a God who offers himself to God? During the consecration, we must beg God the Father for grace through the merits of his only Son Jesus Christ, his Holy Wounds, his most precious Blood and through the tears and sorrows of the Virgin Mary who, as his mother, intercedes for us more than anyone else." At the end of the consecration, Carlo used to repeat: "Through the Sacred Heart of Jesus and the Immaculate Heart of Mary, I present to you all my petitions and I beg you to hear me." He also liked to repeat an ejaculatory prayer that a cloistered monk once taught him: "Wounds of Christ, sources of love and mercy, speak on our behalf in the presence of the Divine Father and obtain for us internal transformation."

After receiving Communion, Carlo was in the habit of saying, "Jesus, make yourself at home! Live within me as if it were your own dwelling!" He also often said, "You can go straight to heaven if you avail yourself of the Eucharist every day!" Once he said, "Jesus is very creative because he hides in a little piece of bread, and only God could do something so incredible!" These words reveal his profound love for the Eucharist. He was only ten years old when he said these words. Despite his youth, he put into practice the mystery celebrated on the altar. His entire life was practically a reflection of the Eucharistic mystery: a self-giving to all for love of Christ. He lived this devotion in freedom and simplicity, with depth, and with no concern for what others thought of him. He never ceased being a fun-loving, enthusiastic boy with lots of friends, but he did so with his heart turned constantly to God. With the passing of years, his love for Christ increased exponentially. When he was unable to attend Mass because of his illness, he never failed to make a spiritual communion.

Carlo became a true apostle of the Eucharist to his friends and classmates, especially in his mission to teach them about the most famous Eucharistic miracles in the history of Christendom. He also told the stories of the lives of mystics who were especially devoted to the Eucharist, such as Blessed Alexandrina Maria Da Costa, who lived in Balasar, Portugal. Paralyzed and confined to her bed, Blessed Alexandrina consumed nothing but the consecrated Host for thirteen years. Carlo was amazed at everything the Lord revealed to Alexandrina: "I put you in the world, and I am allowing you to subsist only on me to prove to the world the infinite worth of the Eucharist and what it means for me to live in souls: It is a light of salvation for all humanity. I have been so forgotten! Indeed, I am offended! I wish to be loved in the Holy Eucharist: It is the source of all grace!"

Both Carlo's spiritual director and his pastor in Centola were convinced that he would have become a priest some day. They had seen clear evidence of a vocation. His pastor was convinced that there was something that distinguished him from his peers: "What immediately caught my attention — because you don't see many kids doing it — was Carlo's participation at daily Mass, which he always attended with prayer and love. His life in the Church, courageous Christian witness, simplicity, peace, joy, and affability toward all were the fruits that clearly showed he rooted his life in faith and nourished it with God's grace."

Another sign of Carlo's devotion to the Eucharist was his habit of spending long hours in prayer in front of the tabernacle. This was his privileged time of silent adoration in "the true presence of the Body and Blood of Our Lord Jesus Christ, just as he was present when he lived on earth in Palestine." He willingly spent time adoring the Lord he loved so much and by whom he felt infinitely loved and cared for. His certainty of being loved by the Holy Trinity pulled him into the Trinitarian love and pushed him ever more deeply into the Eucharistic mystery. He used to say to his parents: "Jesus Christ took on flesh to come to us and save us both from original sin inherited from our first parents and the sins each of us commits every day — even involuntarily — because unfortunately we are limited. But the Eucharist is nothing other than the heavenly food that keeps us out of temptation. When in the Lord's Prayer we say, 'give us this day our daily bread, and lead us not into temptation,' Jesus meant, 'give us today the daily Eucharist.'"

The time Carlos spent with the Most Holy Sacrament enflamed his desire to give himself unreservedly and completely to Christ the Lamb sacrificed for all humanity. His prayer in front of the tabernacle increased his love for Jesus and transformed him into an authentic apostle not only in word, but in his way of life. This is evident in one of his meditations: "The Lord Jesus took on flesh by choosing a poor fifteen-year-old girl as his mother and a carpenter as his adoptive father. When he was born, a lot of people refused to let him in because they didn't know where to put him, but someone finally found him a barn." Carlo used to say that if we think about it, the manger in Bethlehem "was certainly better than a lot of houses that refuse to let the Lord in today or betray him, because he is received unworthily. A poor fifteen-year-old girl and a poor carpenter became the parents of God, who chose poverty rather than riches. I think this is absolutely incredible!" Once, Carlo's father asked him to join him on a pilgrimage to the Holy Land organized by one of his priest-friends. Carlo had a disarming response: "I prefer to stay here in Milan because there are so many tabernacles where I can visit Jesus at any time, so I don't feel the need to go to Jerusalem. We have Jerusalem right out our front door." To be even more precise, he added: "If Jesus stays with us wherever there is a consecrated Host, what need is there to go on pilgrimage to Jerusalem to visit the places he lived two thousand years ago? If only people visited tabernacles with the same devotion!"

We can only imagine how struck Carlo's father was by these affirmations that revealed such deep Eucharistic devotion in Carlo's soul. Carlo's spiritual director also testifies to Carlo's abiding love for the Most Holy Sacrament: "He went to Eucharistic adoration several times a week, and every time I met him, he would tell me of the advances he had made through this practice. Shortly before he died, I hosted him in Bologna, and he told me that he had made a lot of progress in Eucharistic adoration. He explained that he was finally able to remain undistracted during adoration and that — thanks to his time in adoration — his love for the Lord had grown enormously."

He often dedicated periods of Eucharistic adoration to pray for sinners and the souls in purgatory. Someone explained to Carlo that by praying for at least half an hour in front of the Eucharist, he could obtain a plenary indulgence from the Church under the usual conditions. He therefore used this prayer time to help many souls in need as he applied the indulgences gained to souls in purgatory.

SOME EUCHARISTIC MIRACLES
The Eucharistic Miracle of Lanciano, Italy, c. 750

A marble inscription from the seventeenth century in the Church of Saint Francis describes the Eucharistic Miracle that occurred in Lanciano in 750 "A monastic priest doubted whether the consecrated host was really the Body of our Lord. He celebrated Mass and, once he had pronounced the words of consecration, he witnessed the bread become flesh and the wine become blood. He showed everyone present what had happened. The flesh is still intact and the blood is divided into five unequal parts that weigh the same regardless of whether they are placed on a scale separately or together."

In 1970, the archbishop of Lanciano and the provincial of the conventual friars in Abruzzo, with authorization from Rome, asked Doctor Edoardo Linoli, director of the hospital in Arezzo and a professor of anatomy, histology, chemistry, and clinical microscopy, to perform a scientific examination of the relics from the miracle that had occurred twelve centuries earlier. On March 4, 1971, the professor presented the results of his extensive research. Here are his essential conclusions:

1. The "miraculous flesh" consists of human myocardial striated muscular tissue.
2. The "miraculous blood" is true blood, as definitively and indisputably proven by chromographic analysis.
3. Immunographical studies show that the body and blood are undoubtedly human in nature, and immunohematological tests prove with objective certainty that both belong to the same blood-type group AB, which corresponds to the

analyses carried out on the Shroud of Turin. The blood-type broadly corresponds to peoples from the middle East.

4. The proteins contained in the blood are distributed normally according to the exact percentages of serum proteins in a fresh, normal cell.

5. Histological analyses revealed no traces of infiltrations of salts or other preservative substances used in ancient times for the purposes of mummification.

These results, published in the *Quaderni Sclavo in Diagnostica* (fasc. 3, 1971), caught much attention in the scientific community. Again in 1973 the Consiglio superiore dell'Organizzazione Mondiale della Sanità appointed a scientific commission to verify Linoli's conclusions. More precisely, it was affirmed that the fragments preserved in Lanciano were incomparable to mummified tissue. Regarding the fragment of flesh, the commission declared that it behaved like living flesh in that it immediately responded to all the clinical reactions that would be expected from living organisms. The flesh and blood of Lanciano thus showed characteristics of flesh having been sampled from a living being on that very day. In a summary report of the Medical Commission of the Italian Ministry of Health and of the United Nations published in 1976 in New York and Geneva, it was declared that science — within its known limits — could not explain these phenomena.

The Eucharistic Miracle of Buenos Aires, Argentina, 1992, 1994, 1996

The parish of Santa Maria in Buenos Aires was the site of no fewer than three Eucharistic miracles occurring in 1992,

1994, and 1996. Professor Ricardo Castañón Gómez was summoned by the then archbishop of Buenos Aires — who was none other than the future Pope Francis — to analyze the miracle that had occurred on August 15, 1996.

As one of the Eucharistic ministers was attending to the remaining hosts after Mass on May 1, 1992, he found a piece of the consecrated Host on the corporal. Following the norms of the Church, the priest asked him to place it in a container of water which was in turn placed in the tabernacle to dissolve it. In the following days, when various priests went to the tabernacle to check on it, they were surprised to find that nothing had changed. Seven days later, on Friday, May 8, they opened the tabernacle and saw that the fragments had turned a reddish color resembling blood. On the following Sunday, May 10, during evening Mass, they noticed small drops of blood on the paten that the priests were using to distribute Communion. On July 24, 1994, during the Mass for children, while the Eucharistic minister was taking the pix from the tabernacle, he saw a drop of blood running along the sides of the tabernacle. On August 15, 1996, during the Mass for the Assumption of the Most Holy Virgin, another fragment of the Sacred Host had to be placed in water to dissolve because it had fallen to the floor during the distribution of Communion. A few days later, on August 26, a minister of the Eucharist opened the tabernacle to find that the host had been transformed into blood.

This is the testimony signed by Professor Castañón regarding the Eucharistic miracle that occurred in 1996 in the parish of Santa Maria: "On August 15, 1996, a consecrated Host accidentally fell from the hands of a member of the faithful during Communion time, but he decided not to pick it up because it seemed 'dirty.' Another attendee noticed what had happened, picked up the Host, and put it in a safe place. This person explained to Father Alejandro Pezet what had happened. Following the Church's liturgical norms, the priest placed the Host into a container of water which he then put into the tabernacle to dissolve it.

"When the tabernacle was opened on August 26 to check the Host, it had not completely dissolved but showed some red splotches that grew a little every day. The parish priests immediately contacted the Archbishop of Buenos Aires to report what had happened. It was decided that we should wait a few days before opening up the scientific analyses, and in 1999, the Archbishop — after learning that the analyses were being performed free of charge — asked me to oversee the procedures. On October 6, 1999, I went to Buenos Aires to interview the five priests who had witnessed the incident, and it was then that they told me they had similarly seen a host turn bloody in May 1992. They had placed it in distilled water, which is the worst way to preserve anything, and this really worried me. Everyone knows that when you extract blood, it is possible to take a leukocyte count (i.e., count of white blood cells). Within the blood, there is a variety of white blood cells with certain specific characteristics. The priests knew a woman chemist in the parish whom they asked to analyze the bloody Host. She ascertained that it was human blood and that the entire leukocyte count was accurate. She was surprised to discover that the white blood cells were active. The chemist could not, however, perform a genetic test on the sample since it was very difficult to carry out a test at that time. She extracted a specimen from the two hosts which had turned bloody in the presence of the archdiocesan notary, who certified the legality of the action as the authorities of the Argentinian church requested. I want to clarify that before he invited me, the Archbishop of Buenos Aires had already contacted the Holy See to seek approval for my handling of the case. This was granted by His Excellency Gianfranco Girotti, who was then Under Secretary at the Congregation for the Doctrine of the Faith and a close collaborator of Cardinal Ratzinger. On October 21, I visited the genetics laboratory at Forence Analytical di San Francisco, where the sample I had brought was being tested. On January 28, they had found fragments of human DNA in the sample, meaning the blood was human with a genetic code. In March 2000, I was informed that Doctor Robert Lawrence, one of the most famous legal histopathologists, had been involved in the analysis. I was concerned about his involvement because I imagined I would be responsible for a hefty fee, but I was told that they themselves had requested his collaboration since they had found substances resembling human tissue. Doctor Lawrence studied the samples and found human skin cells and white blood cells. In December 2000, Doctor Lawrence told me that he could have obtained other samples of DNA as well.

"In 2001, I took the samples to Professor Linoli who identified the presence of white blood cells and told me that it was highly likely that these samples contained human cardiac tissue. The results of the analysis on the samples were quite similar to the results of the studies done on the Lanciano miraculous Host. In 2002, we sent the sample to Professor John Walker of the University of Sydney in Australia, who confirmed that the samples consisted of muscular cells and intact white blood cells, and everyone knows that white blood cells that have been outside of the body for fifteen minutes will disintegrate, and in this case, we are dealing with a specimen already six years old.

"In September 2003, I went to visit Professor Robert Lawrence again, and he confirmed for me that the new analyses revealed that the specimen was composed of swollen cardiac material. This suggested that the person from whom it came had suffered greatly. To remove any remaining doubts, on March 2, 2004, we went to visit the world's leading cardiac pathologist and forensic medicine expert, Professor Frederick Zugibe of Columbia University in New York. The Professor, however, did not know that the sample had been taken from the consecrated Host. The professor told me that the sample consisted of myocardial muscular tissue taken from the left ventricle, and that the patient from whom the sample had been taken must have suffered intensely. So, I asked him, 'Doctor, why do you say that the patient suffered greatly?' He responded, 'Because this patient had blood clots. He must not have been able to breathe at times. He wasn't getting enough oxygen. Every breath must have been painful for him and he must have been utterly exhausted. He probably received some blow to the chest. Furthermore, the heart must have been dynamically active (i.e., living) at the moment when you brought me the sample. We found intact white blood cells which can only be transported in the bloodstream, so if there were white blood cells present it can only be because you brought it to me while it was still beating.' The professor then asked to whom the sample belonged. When we told him it came from a consecrated Host, he said, 'I don't believe it.' He was utterly stunned. The professor then showed us a book in which was recorded the case of one of his patients who had lesions very similar to those in the sample we had brought him. The myocardial muscle is the muscle that gives life to our entire heart and organism. A theologian mentioned to me that it was no accident that myocardial tissue was involved in the miracle, for the Lord wanted to show us the muscle that gives life to the entire heart, just as the Eucharist gives life to the heart of the Church. And why the left ventricle? Because this is the source of purified blood, just as Jesus is the one who purifies the Church of her sins. The doctor told me that the moment I brought the sample in, the heart must have been alive! This report was mailed on March 26, 2005, five and a half years after the studies began. The conclusions were these: 'The sample consists of cardiac tissue of a heart that suffered degenerative changes in the myocardia, and these changes were due to the fact that the cells were inflamed, and the sample comes from the left ventricle.' The results of the study were brought to Cardinal Jorge Maria Bergoglio on March 17, 2006."

The Eucharistic Miracle of Tixtla, Mexico, 2006

On October 12, 2013, his excellency Alejo Zavala Castro, bishop of the Diocese of Chilpancingo-Chilapa, published a pastoral letter announcing a Eucharistic miracle that took place in Tixtla on October 21, 2006. The bishop wrote: "This is a wonderful manifestation of God's love since it confirms the real presence of Jesus in the Eucharist ... in my role as the bishop of this diocese, I acknowledge the supernatural character of the series of events surrounding the bleeding Host of Tixtla. ... I declare it to be a 'Divine Sign.'"

On October 21, 2006, during a Eucharistic celebration in Tixtla — a village within the Diocese of Chilpancingo-Chilapa — a red blood-like substance began to ooze from the consecrated Host. The bishop, his excellency Alejo Zavala Castro, convened a theological commission to study the case. In October 2009, he invited Doctor Ricardo Castañón Gómez to assume direction of the scientific research aimed at clarifying what had happened. The Mexican ecclesiastical authorities called on Doctor Castañón Gómez because they knew that from 1999 to 2006, he was involved in the scientific analyses of the two consecrated hosts that had secreted blood at the parish of Santa Maria in Buenos Aires.

The Mexican case began in October 2006 when Father Leopoldo Roque, pastor of the parish of Saint Martin of Tours, invited Father Raymundo Reyna Esteban to lead a spiritual retreat for parishioners. Father Leopoldo, another priest, and a nun were distributing Communion. At a certain point the nun, who was standing to the left of Father Leopoldo, showed him a Host she had taken from the ciborium to administer to one of the faithful. She had tears in her eyes. Father Leopoldo noticed that the Host had begun to secrete a reddish substance. Indeed, it had begun to bleed.

"The ecclesiastical authorities desire to make clear that the Eucharistic miracle is remarkable for the following reasons.

1. Theological: The miracle came about by divine intervention.
2. Objectivity: The alteration of natural causes or laws is clearly evident.
3. Subjectivity: Whoever accepts the miracle 'acknowledges or accepts' by an act of faith that this extraordinary event proceeded from the loving will of our Creator.
4. End: It has as its purpose the good of one or several persons."

The scientific studies conducted between October 2009 and October 2012 led to the following conclusions that were presented on May 25, 2013, during an international symposium in the Diocese of Chilpancingo to celebrate the Year of Faith:

1. The red substance secreted from the host consists of blood proven to be human by hemoglob-

ular and genetic analysis.

2. Two studies conducted by well-respected forensic experts using different methodologies demonstrated that the substance was secreted from within, thus excluding the possibility that someone could have applied it to the outside.

3. The blood type is AB, similar to that discovered in the Lanciano host and the Shroud of Turin.

4. Microscopic analysis reveals that the upper section of the secretion had coagulated sometime in October 2006. But in February 2010, the lower sections showed signs of fresh blood.

5. The presence of intact white blood cells and red blood cells was detected, as well as macrophages actively consuming lipids. The tissue in question appears lacerated and in a state of self-repair just as would be expected in living tissue.

6. Further histopathological analysis identified the presence of protein-based structures in a state of deterioration, suggesting the presence of mesenchymal cells which are notable for their high level of biophysiological activity.

7. Immunohistochemical studies reveal that the tissue in question corresponds to heart (i.e., myocardial) muscle.

Given the results of these scientific studies and the conclusions of the theological commission, on October 12 the bishop of Chilpancingo, Alejo Zavala Castro, announced the following: "The occurrence has no natural explanation. It is not rooted in paranormal activity. It cannot be attributed to manipulation by an enemy force."

The Eucharistic Miracle of Sokółka, Poland, 2008

On October 12, 2008, a young priest named Father Filip Zdrodowski, associate pastor of Saint Anthony Parish in Sokółka, celebrated Mass at 8:30 a.m. One of the priests accidently dropped a Host during the distribution of Communion. He hadn't even noticed. One of the women kneeling to receive Communion pointed it out to him. The priest froze, and fearing it had been spoiled, he placed it in a small, silver container containing water that priests normally use to wash their fingers after distributing Holy Communion. At the end of Mass, the sacristan, Sister Julia Dubowska, took the container with the Host and, in order to keep it safe, poured it into another container that would fit into the locked cabinet where chalices were kept.

One week later, on October 19, around 8:00 a.m., the sister opened the container and found that the Host was almost dissolved, but in the center, she found a strange, red coagulated substance. She immediately summoned the priests to show them what had happened. The Host itself was mostly dissolved. There was only a small piece of the consecrated Host firmly connected to the red substance on its surface. That is, a small part of the Host was connected to that "strange coagulated red substance." The pastor then contacted the Metropolitan Curia in Białystok. The archbishop, Edward Ozorowski, together with the chancellor of the curia, the priest, and some professors examined the Host, and baffled, they decided to wait for awhile to see if and how things would develop. On October 29, the container with the Host was brought to the parish chapel and enclosed in the tabernacle there. The next day, following the orders of the archbishop, Father Gniedziejko removed the partially dissolved Host and the attached red substance from the container with a small spoon and placed it on a white corporal with a red cross stitched in the center. The corporal was then folded, placed in a container, and returned to the tabernacle in such a way that it could be transported when necessary. After a while, the host "gelled" with the corporal and the "coagulated red substance" dried. It was only then that two world-class scientists, specialists in pathological anatomy, were called in from the Medical University of Białystok. The Metropolitan Curia in Białystok then released this statement regarding the Eucharistic miracle occurring in Sokółka:

1. On October 12, 2008, a consecrated Host fell from the hands of a priest while distributing Holy Communion. He picked it up and placed it in a container of water, which he then placed in the tabernacle. After Mass, the vessel containing the host was placed in a locked cupboard in the sacristy.

2. On October 19, 2008, when the locked cupboard was opened, a red mark could clearly be seen on the Host that had fallen, which with the naked eye clearly appeared to be blood.

3. On October 29, 2008, the container with the Host was moved to the tabernacle of the chapel in the rectory. On the next day, the Host was removed from the container of water and placed on a corporal which was, in turn, put into the tabernacle.

4. On January 7, 2009, a sample of the Host was removed and examined independently by two professional histopathologists at the Medical University of Białystok. They subsequently released a joint statement in which they said: "The sample sent for evaluation was myocardi-

al tissue. In our opinion, it resembles this type of tissue more than anything else."

5. The Commission certified that the Host that had been analyzed was the same that had been moved from the sacristy to the tabernacle in the chapel of the rectory. No third party was involved.

6. There was nothing in the Sokółka case that contradicted the Church's teaching. Indeed, it affirmed it.

Toward the beginning of 2009, the Curia in Białystok asked two prominent specialists in pathological anatomy at the Medical University of Białystok — Professor Maria Elzbieta Sobaniec-Łotowska and Professor Stanisław Sulkowski — to analyze samples of the blood-stained Host. On January 7, Professor Sobaniec-Łotowska went to Sokółka and extracted a tiny sample of the mysterious substance present on the Host.

The professors stressed that numerous bio-morphological signs were found in the sample indicating the presence of cardial muscular tissue: for example, the phenomenon of segmentation, or damage to the cardial muscular tissues found at intercellular junctions (these are structures characteristic of cardiac muscle), and the phenomenon of fragmentation. This damage was visible in the form of numerous, minuscule lesions. Such alterations can only be found in neocrotic tissue — that is, living tissue — showing signs of quick spasms in the cardiac muscle that are typical of an organism in the final phases of life before death. Another important piece of evidence is the fact that the analyzed material corresponded to human cardiac muscular tissue with the nucleus positioned centrally in the cells — a typical feature of the heart's muscle fibers. "Along some of the fibers could be seen signs that could correspond to nodes of contraction. However, microscopic analysis revealed the outlines of communicative junctions and myofibrils," the scientists from Białystok announced. Furthermore, the cardiac tissue was attached to the consecrated Host in an unbreakable way. In their report, professors Sobaniec-Łotowska and Sulkowski state: "The results of the analysis were remarkably clear. They indicate that the sample consists of cardiac muscular tissue, and furthermore, that the tissue resembles that of a living organism." "Most importantly, the material analyzed consists completely of cardiac muscular tissue." The latter affirmation was contained in the "Communication of the Metropolitan Curia of Białystok" dated October 14, 2009, regarding the Eucharistic phenomena in Sokółka. The professors also found other inexplicable elements: "The Host remained immersed in water for a long time and on the corporal even longer. The tissue that appeared on the Host therefore should have undergone a process of autolysis; that is, a process of self-destruction carried out by intracellular enzymes. But in the material analyzed there were no traces of this kind of alteration!" Another important observation was that the substance on the corporal, even though it changed slightly after being extracted from water (it was simply dried) a couple of years earlier, did not change in appearance even though it was not preserved in a temperature-controlled environment. "This means that if the miracle was due to the action of some bacteria, it would have disintegrated and would have changed in appearance. Usually, a microbial culture, even when placed on a sterilized area, will appear completely changed after a week," Professor Sulkowski added.

"Initially, I was convinced it was a clot," said Professor Sobaniec-Łotowska. But the reality was quite surprising! The two Białystok scientists used the most modern microscopic technology available and arrived at the same conclusion (Professor Sulkowski did not know that the sample came from a Eucharistic Host). The sample examined was neither a clot nor blood. Rather, it was living human cardiac muscular tissue. And, even more incredibly, it was cardiac muscle with the typical indications of the last phase before death.

There were some people who had neither analyzed the material nor had ever seen it with their eyes, but who claimed that the red color of the host was due to prodigiosin, a red pigment produced by the bacterium Serratia marcescens. "This is obviously absurd," the two Białystok specialists stated, adding that the observed material corresponded to cardiac muscle and not to a bacterium. The Białystok scientists analyzed the sample merely on a scientific basis, not on the basis of faith. There were even more absurd accusations, such as those advanced by a group of so-called "rationalists" who claimed that the analyzed tissue belonged to an assassinated individual. The professors reacted by making a statement in which they expressed "deep regret for the fact that public opinion had been falsely swayed by the false, pseudoscientific hypotheses regarding the analyzed tissue, especially by people who ignored the specifics of the analysis, had never had access to the material, had never consulted the written documentation, and often were not even familiar with the technical aspects of the applied analyses." It took the scientists two weeks to prepare the official report.

When the diocesan curia in Białystok was made aware of the incredible results of the analysis, a special ecclesiastical commission was appointed by the archbishop on March 30, 2009. It was entrusted with the task of examining the miracle from a theological point of view and interviewing everyone who had seen the Host and who could serve as a witness to the extraordinary events. It was also the commission's duty to expel any doubt of mystification and to affirm that no one had secretly substituted the Host in the tabernacle with something else. The members of the commission — composed of distinguished professors from the seminary in Białystok — questioned every witness and ascertained the truth of the testimony. The ecclesiastical commission finally produced the following declaration:

"The host from which the sample was taken for analysis is precisely the same host that had been transferred from the sacristy to the tabernacle in the chapel of the rectory. There was absolutely no third party involved."

This was also categorically denied by the two scientists from Białystok. It is not possible for anyone to have placed a fragment of human flesh into the tabernacle. What does that leave? The remaining fragments of the Host were closely connected to the human tissue fibers, intimately bound to them, as if a fragment of "bread" at a certain point had evolved into "flesh." It is impossible to perform this kind of act through manipulation. No one, absolutely no one, could have affected something of this nature. "Even NASA scientists, who have at their disposal the most advanced instruments of technical analysis, would not have been able to re-create something of this nature artificially," affirmed Professor Sobaniec-Łotowska, adding that the event had had a particular impact on her own life.

The Eucharistic Miracle of Legnica, Poland, 2013

In December 2013, in the Church of Saint Hyacinth in Legnica, during the distribution of Communion, a Host inadvertently fell to the floor. It was immediately placed into a container of water, which in turn was put into the tabernacle as directed by Canon Law. Some time later, a red splotch appeared on the surface of the Host. The bishop of Legnica, his excellency Stefan Cichy, immediately decided to have the host analyzed by a scientific commission. The surprising results of the analysis revealed that the substance was "human cardiac tissue showing signs of extreme physical distress."

The specifics of the case are the following. On December 25, 2013, during the distribution of Communion, a consecrated Host inadvertently fell to the floor. It was immediately placed into a container of water. The pastor of Saint Hyacinth, Father Andrzej Ziombra, testified that on January 4 — almost two weeks after the incident — he went with a few other priests to see if the consecrated Host that had fallen had been dissolved by the water. "We immediately noted that the Host had not dissolved and that there was a red mark that covered about one-fifth of its surface. We therefore decided to tell the bishop what had happened, and he decided to appoint a theological-scientific commission to look into the event. In the meantime, we noticed that as more time passed, the mark on the host had changed color and become more intense, almost a reddish-brown. ... A sample of the Host was directly investigated by the scientists on January 26, 2014. The miracle was evident enough to us priests. But the commission had to verify first of all whether the phenomenon could be attributed to some type of fungus, mold, or other foreign substance. ... The initial analysis performed at the Institute of Forensic Medicine in Wrocław immediately ruled out the possibility of bacteria, fungus, or any other red-colored material. The second histopathological analysis revealed that some fragments seemed to consist of myocardial tissue. We subsequently decided to seek further input, so we brought the same sample to the Institute of Forensic Medicine in Szczecin without informing them about the origin of the sample. They decided to use a different method of analysis. After the analysis, the Department of Histopathology at the Pomeranian Medical University in Szczecin released a statement in which they announced that 'histopathological imaging revealed that the sample included fragments of tissue with transverse striation.' The report continued: 'The sample is very similar to human cardiac muscle that has been subjected to extreme stress. We did not analyze the blood found on the Host. We only know that human DNA was found in that sample.' The results of the research were presented to the Congregation for the Doctrine of the Faith which recognized the supernatural character of the event. The results of the examination are strikingly similar to those of the Eucharistic Miracle in Lanciano in A.D. 750, and to other miracles such as those of Sokółka in 2008, Tixtla in 2006, and Buenos Aires in 1996. On April 17, 2016, his excellency Zbigniew Kiernikowskiego, the new bishop of Legnica, announced during Mass that, following the directives of the Holy See, he had asked the pastor of the church, Father Andrzej Ziombra 'to prepare a worthy place for the exposition of the precious reliquary so that the faithful might express adoration in an appropriate way."

The Source and Summit of the Church

Carlo said that "God has written a unique and unrepeatable story for each of us, but he lets us write the ending." How many people write such a bad ending! In order to avoid the risk of writing his life "with a bad ending," Carlo trusted in the Eucharist. For Carlo, the Eucharist was the greatest expression of God's love for us. It was the beacon that sheds light on our entire existence. It is the inspiration that allows us to give our life for our friends just like Jesus did. It is the certainty that, even though Christ now sits in glory at the Father's right hand, he continues to dwell with us sacramentally on earth, offering himself continuously to the Father in the Sacrifice of the Mass.

In 1916, an angel appeared to the visionaries in Fatima — Lucia, Francesco, and Jacinta — holding a chalice in his left hand, over which was suspended a Host from which drops of blood were falling into the chalice. He then asked the children to repeat this prayer three times: "O Most Holy Trinity, Father, Son and Holy Spirit, I adore thee profoundly. I offer thee the most precious Body, Blood, Soul and Divinity of Jesus Christ present in all the tabernacles of the world in reparation for the outrages, sacrileges and indifferences by which he is offended. By the infinite merits of the Sacred Heart of Jesus and the Immaculate Heart of Mary I beg the conversion of poor sinners." Then, arising again, the angel took the chalice with the Host and gave it to Lucia and the chalice containing the blood to Francesco and Jacinta, saying, "Take and receive the Body and Blood of Jesus Christ, horribly betrayed by ungrateful men. Make reparation for their crimes and console your God."

This means that we can unite our pain and sacrifices to those of Christ and thus make reparation for offenses against God. This was an invitation that Carlo accepted and put into practice. In a letter to one of his fellow Capuchins, Padre Pio wrote how the Lord desires to be consoled: "My dear Father, I was still in bed on Friday morning, when Jesus appeared to me. He was battered and disfigured. He showed me a great crowd of priests, including religious and secular clerics, as well as some ecclesiastical dignitaries. Some of them were celebrating Mass, others were preparing to celebrate, and others were unvesting after Mass. Jesus's tortured face really pained me, and I wanted to ask him why he was suffering so much. He gave no answer. But his gaze led me to look at those priests again. A little later, as if horrified and tired of looking at them, he averted his gaze and looked at me again with extreme dismay. I noticed two tears running down his cheeks. Then, turning away from that crowd of priests with deep disgust on his face, he turned to me and said: My son, do not think that my agony lasted three hours. No. Because of these souls that have received so much from me, I will be in agony until the end of time. During this time of agony, my son, there is no time for sleep. My soul will continue to search for even the slightest sense of human pity, but alas, everyone has abandoned me in indifference. The ingratitude and exhaustion of my ministers make my agony even worse. O, how they have responded so poorly to my love! What pains me the most is that they pile disgrace and unbelief on top of indifference."

Saint Gemma Galgani also affirms that Jesus suffers in his Mystical Body because of our sins: "Look at all of the wounds that you have left on Jesus's body because of your sins; you have healed them by your pain." Many other mystics besides Saint Gemma and Padre Pio of Pietrelcina had visions of Jesus suffering.

The same thing can be said of the Mass insofar as it re-presents his sacrifice on the cross in an un-bloody way. Jesus continues to suffer for us and offer himself for us, and he will continue to do so until the end of time. It is true that Jesus is now in heaven and that he possesses infinite joy, but it is also true that he continues to offer himself for us every day in each Mass, and that he consequently "feels" the offenses and sacrileges committed against his sacramental presence.

Regarding reparation, Pius XI writes the following in his encyclical *Miserentissimus Redemptor*: "Now if, because of our sins also which were as yet in the future, but were foreseen, the soul of Christ became sorrowful unto death, it cannot be doubted that then, too, already He derived somewhat of solace from our reparation, which was likewise foreseen, when 'there appeared to Him an angel from heaven' (Lk 22:43), in order that His Heart, oppressed with weariness and anguish, might find consolation. And so even now, in a wondrous yet true manner, we can and ought to console that Most Sacred Heart which is continually wounded by the sins of thankless men, since — as we also read in the sacred liturgy — Christ Himself, by the mouth of the Psalmist complains that He is forsaken by His friends: 'My Heart hath expected reproach and misery, and I looked for one that would grieve together with me, but there was none: and for one that would comfort me, and I found none.'"

Carlo was always moved by the words Jesus left us in the Gospel of Matthew: "I am with you always, to the close of the age" (Mt 28:20). The certainty of God's presence among us was a source of tremendous consolation for Carlo. "We can find God in his Body, Soul, and Divinity present in all the tabernacles of the world! If we think about it, we are much more fortunate than those who met Jesus on this earth two thousand years ago, because we have God 'really and substantially' with us always. It is enough to visit a nearby church. 'Jerusalem' is in every church! No room for despair! God is always with us and will never abandon us. How can people grasp this truth? Throngs of people stand in interminable lines to buy tickets to rock concerts or soccer matches, but I don't see crowds of people lined up outside church waiting to see Jesus in the Eucharist. This should make us pause and reflect. ... Perhaps people really haven't yet understood! Jesus is present among us in his very Body just as he was during his mortal life among his friends. If we reflected on this seriously, we would never leave him alone in the tabernacles waiting for us with love, wanting to help us and to support us on our earthly journey."

Among his many voluntary activities, Carlo decided to help his pastor by teaching catechesis, and it was this experience that inspired him to put together an exhibit on Eucharistic miracles recognized by the Church. The exhibit took almost two and half years to put together and involved the collaboration of many friends. The fruits of this exhibition have been incredible. It still travels the world after traveling across five continents and stopping at important shrines such as Fatima and Guadalupe. Carlo was well aware that people are primarily concerned with material things, and they risked losing their sense of the supernatural and the immense riches the Lord has given us in the sacraments. Carlo used to say, "Our frenetic pace of life has made us forget that each of us must climb Golgotha sooner or later. Our journey on this earth is marked from the beginning: We are all invited to take up our cross and climb Golgotha." He also stated, "Our lives will truly be beautiful only if we discover how to love God above all things and our neighbor as ourselves." To do this, we need God's help in the sacraments, especially the Eucharist. This is why Carlo spent so much time trying to convince others of the importance of this sacrament: "Jesus is Love, and he has made himself food and drink for us in the Eucharist. The more we nourish ourselves on the Body, Blood, Soul, and Divinity of Christ, the more we will be able to love. ... The Eucharist configures us in a special way to God, who is Love."

Furthermore, we will become saints only if we are able to "love God above all things, and our neighbor as ourselves." And what could help us more to reach this ultimate objective than the very source of Love, who gives us himself in the Eucharist? As Saint Paul writes, "Love never ends." When we die, everything else will pass away, and we will be judged by

God solely on how much we have loved him, and we will be able to place him first and foremost in our lives only to the extent that we have loved our neighbor.

Through the Eucharist, we unite ourselves ever more closely to Christ and we assimilate his thoughts and feelings, enabling us to practice the virtues that he taught and modeled for us ever more heroically, just as Saint Paul exhorts, "Have this mind among yourselves, which was in Christ Jesus" (Phil 2:5).

Carlo always had a close relationship with Saint John the Apostle, the disciple loved and favored by God, who rested his head on Christ's heart at the Last Supper: the heart that the Church has always recognized in a special way in the Eucharist. Carlo always saw this as a special invitation to men and women of all time to become true disciples of Christ. We could say that John is a prefigurement of the "beloved disciple" within all of us. He is a sign of God's universal call to everyone to follow him and to become his intimate friends. With that simple gesture of reclining his head on the Heart of Christ — a symbol of the Eucharist — John continues to exhort us to join him in becoming intimate friends with Jesus through an intense Eucharistic life. Carlo used to say that God gives every human being the potential to become a saint, but it is up to us to put God's utterly unique plan for us into action: a plan he created at the beginning of time. We are all called to join John in becoming beloved disciples, united to the Eucharistic Heart of Jesus.

Carlo deeply pondered the Eucharistic miracle of Lanciano where the consecrated Host was transformed into human flesh that turned out to be myocardial tissue, i.e., the muscle forming the walls of the heart, whose task it is to allow the heart to contract and push blood to the rest of the body. Just as the heart is the organ that gives life to the rest of the organism, so the Eucharist gives life to the entire Church: "The Eucharist is the source and summit of the Christian life." In fact, we read in the *Catechism of the Catholic Church*: "The other sacraments, and indeed all ecclesiastical ministries and works of the apostolate, are bound up with the Eucharist and are oriented toward it. For the blessed Eucharist contains the whole spiritual good of the Church, namely Christ himself, our Pasch" (1324). In recent times, the Lord desires to call attention to this incredible reality through his Eucharistic miracles.

Finally, Carlo teaches us that this call to become intimate friends with Jesus through an encounter with him in the Eucharist is even more evident in the story of the crucifixion. Beneath the cross on Golgotha, in addition to Mary and the other women, we meet John, the beloved disciple, who stayed after the others fled. Here, too, John shows us that the Eucharist is the privileged means of uniting ourselves to God.

"If we reflect deeply on this reality, the Gospel story teaches us that the sacrifice on the cross which occurred two thousand years ago is just as present to us in all the Masses celebrated today. Just like John, we can unite ourselves to the sacrifice on the cross and show our love for God by participating in Mass every day. We cannot ignore Jesus' invitation to unite ourselves with him."

Carlo found a passage in the *Lineamenta* for the Eleventh Ordinary General Assembly of the Synod of Bishops in 2005 that sums up his understanding of the Eucharist: "The Eucharist ... expresses the participation of the People of God, its movement towards the heavenly Church, culminating in the *Sanctus*, the hymn of victory, a blending of the angel's hymn in the vision of Isaiah and the acclamation of the people of Jerusalem to the Lord, who entered the Holy City to give himself freely to his passion."

CONFESSION

Carlo's devotion to the Eucharist instilled in his heart an equal desire to make use confession, the Sacrament of Reconciliation. In accord with the suggestions of his spiritual director, he went to confession weekly and strove continuously to cooperate with the Lord's grace and unite himself ever more closely to Jesus. He was intent on strengthening himself in those areas where he was weakest: gluttony, idle chatter, and distractions during the Rosary. He often went to confession to Father Mario Perego, a priest at his parish. Father Perego's words attest to the progresses that Carlo made in uniting himself to Christ: "He was exceptionally transparent and forthright. He always wanted to become more perfect in every area of his life: loving his parents, who taught him how to love God; actively participating in community meetings and attending Mass on Sunday; being a better friend to his schoolmates; applying himself more seriously to studies, especially computer science, the humanities, and religion. In order to thank the Lord and to seek encouragement to become better, he went to the Sacrament of Reconciliation weekly, happy to hear the Church's words of forgiveness. Even though he was called to the Lord's glory at such a young age, my memories of Carlo are so vivid that I can feel his concrete help in my own discernment."

His spiritual director also attests to the importance of confession in Carlo's life: "He came to see me in Bologna every month, and he always asked me to hear his confession. He had such a keen judgment of his weaknesses, and was intent on confessing even the smallest of sins."

His frequent confession was a grace to remove the obstacles that impeded his spiritual progress, as he explained with this metaphor: "Even the smallest defect keeps us stuck to this earth like a helium balloon grasped lightly between two fingers."

Carlo used another simile to help us understand the necessity of confession: "In order to climb higher, a hot-air balloon needs to shed weight, just as a soul needs to shed itself of venial sins to ascend to heaven. If one happens to fall into mortal sin, the soul falls to earth, and confession is like the fire that reinflates the balloon and allows it to ascend once more to heaven. We need to go to confession often because the soul is a very complex reality."

Carlo was an avid reader. He was particularly interested in books on the lives of the saints from which he drew ideas for carrying out his apostolate and evangelizing. There are two saints whom he found particularly striking: Saints John Bosco and Francis of Assisi, both of whom drew attention to the danger of dying in a state of mortal sin. Carlo was convinced that people do not reflect enough on the damage inflicted by sin, let alone the risk of dying in mortal sin. He would often say, "If people really recognized the risk involved in breaking God's commandments, they would be much warier of committing serious sins, and they would try harder to admonish their brothers and sisters who live in a way that betrays the baptism they have received."

At the same time, Carlo also learned to recognize that God's mercy is infinite and embraces every creature without distinction. Ever since the year 2000, when John Paul II introduced the feast of Divine Mercy on the first Sunday after Easer — traditionally called *Domenica in albis* — Carlo convinced his parents to join him in observing the Novena of Divine Mercy that the Lord entrusted to Sister Faustina Kowalska with the promise: "I desire that the first Sunday after Easter be the Feast of Mercy. My daughter, tell the whole world about My inconceivable mercy. I desire that the Feast of Mercy be a refuge and shelter for all souls, especially for poor sinners. On that day the very depths of My tender mercy are open. I pour out a whole ocean of graces upon those souls who approach the Fount of My Mercy. The soul that goes to Confession and receives Holy Communion shall obtain complete forgiveness of sins and punishment. On that day, all the divine floodgates through which graces flow are opened. Let no soul fear to draw near to Me, even though its sins be as scarlet."

Carlo was intent on participating in this novena regularly as an antidote to purgatory, just as he had learned from the writings of Catherine of Genoa and Faustina Kowalska. He also read accounts of other saints who had experienced visions of purgatory. He used to say, "If — as the Scriptures affirm, and as the Fatima apparitions confirm in a stunning way — souls really run the risk of eternal damnation, I marvel that hardly anyone ever talks about hell, because it is such a terrible and frightening reality. It sends shivers down my spine just thinking about it." Carlo learned the importance of knowing that this earthly life will come to an end someday, and only God knows when. His father said, "My son lived a completely normal life, but he was remarkable in remembering that, sooner or later, he would die." In fact, when people brought up anything about the future, Carlo would often respond, "Sure, as long as we are still around, because God alone knows how long we have on this earth."

Carlo was aware of the importance of living in a state of grace to be saved, and this always inspired him to live a more committed life of discipleship. He regularly met people who didn't believe in hell or purgatory. Furthermore, he always had a great reverence and respect for priests, even if they didn't model an exemplary life. The maturity of his faith was recognized by everyone. Whenever anyone was irreverent toward the Church, Carlo would interject, "If you criticize the Church, you are simply criticizing yourself."

THE VIRGIN MARY

The other great column of Carlo's faith life was the Virgin Mary, to whom he prayed every day. He once remarked to his parents, "Our Lady is the only lady in my life!" and he never missed "the most important appointment of the day," which was his recitation of the Rosary. He committed himself to her as his Mother and Teacher who taught him to live more perfectly as a disciple of the Lord Jesus. He felt deeply loved by Mary, and he had a burning desire to reciprocate that love. He renewed his consecration to her Immaculate Heart several times during his life, begging her help and protection in his desire to follow her Son as a disciple. His commitment to praying the Rosary daily led to a deep fondness for the Shrine of Our Lady of the Rosary in Pompei. It was a sacred place very dear to his maternal grandfather's family. In fact, his great-grandmother was married there and had made a vow to recite the Rosary every day for the rest of her life. Carlo had heard his relatives talk about his great-grandmother's deep Marian devotion, and this instilled in him a desire to visit the shrine whenever possible. One day, kneeling in front of the image of the Virgin of Pompei, he prayed for the conversion of a certain woman, the mother of a dear family friend, who had given up the sacraments thirty years previously. This woman eventually went to confession, received Holy Communion, and returned to the practice of the Christian Faith. Carlo attributed this conversion to the intercession of the Virgin, and it convinced him that one can obtain any grace by turning to Mary.

He eventually wanted to deepen his consecration to Our Lady by adopting a prayer that priests routinely recite in the sacristy. He was accustomed to saying this prayer of dedication to Mary seven times in a row. He also renewed his consecration to Mary in the presence of a priest after Mass in a church located on Via Sant'Antonio. He received a medal with a golden ribbon to commemorate the dedication. Carlo considered this one of his most cherished possessions. He also encouraged some cousins in Rome who had come to celebrate the New Year with him in Milan to make an act of consecration to Mary.

The Virgin of Pompei was not the only Marian devotion that Carlo practiced. He was also devoted to the apparitions of Mary in Lourdes and Fatima. His parents took him on a tour of Spain in 2005. Carlo insisted that they also go to Lourdes to see where Mary appeared to Bernadette Soubirous so that he could drink water from the grotto. Carlo was very struck by the words Mary said to Saint Bernadette. The fact that Mary would appear to someone like her convinced Carlo that God had a special love for simple, humble people. When he was six, he shared with his parents a locution that he experienced in his soul: "Not self-love, but God's glory." One of the first rosaries Carlo owned was given to him by a distant aunt in Ireland. It bore the symbols of Lourdes. Carlo often carried it with him when traveling. His maternal grandmother, Luana, would often accompany his family when they traveled, and she spotted the rosary. She asked her grandson to tell her about the apparitions. He immediately began to explain the details of the apparitions, noting that, though Bernadette was completely illiterate, she was able to recount everything Our Lady did and said, including when she referred to herself as the Immaculate Conception: a dogma affirmed by Pope Pius IX on December 8, 1854, with the papal bull *Ineffabilis Deus,* four years before the apparitions in Lourdes. It was at the grotto that Carlo made a vow to the Virgin Mary to remain faithful to his recitation of the Rosary every day, a promise he kept throughout his life. He bought some figures of Our Lady that he filled with water from the miraculous font so that he could give some to his parents and to some cloistered nuns he knew. His mother filled several ten-liter bottles with water since they had room in the car.

Briciola, Carlo's favorite dog, was also on the journey. The three-month old puppy was carried in his grandmother's purse. Briciola got involved in a humorous incident when they were visiting the museum at the Descalzas Reales monastery run by the Poor Claires. Their guide told them that pets were not allowed inside the museum. But Carlo's grandmother, Luana, decided to hide him in her purse rather than leave him back at the hotel. The tour took a very long time and had several silent pauses, during which Briciola would start to whimper. Luana coughed continuously to cover up the pooch's pleas. Carlo filmed the entire hilarious episode with his camera.

Carlo also cultivated a strong devotion to the Virgin of Fatima. Carlo himself was baptized in a London church known for its famous statue of Our Lady of Fatima. His entire family was also strongly devoted to the Virgin of Fatima. In 2006, his parents took him to visit the famous Portuguese shrine. He had always desired to see the places where Mary appeared to the three shepherd children Francesco, Jacinta, and Lucia, who had always been an inspiration to him. He was particularly struck by their willingness to make small sacrifices for the love of God. He tried to imitate them by giving up little things like chocolate and movies. He made these little sacrifices with the intention of offering "a bouquet of roses to Our Lady so that she could use him to help her children most in need."

Carlo knew virtually everything about the apparitions of Fatima and never tired of telling others the story. During the pilgrimage he made with his parents, he met the vice-postulator for the cause of Francesco and Jacinta, Father Louis Kondor. His outstanding guides in Fatima were sisters of the Congregation of Mãe de Deus and friends of his mother. They showed him an exhibition on the lives of the children which had been installed at the house that served as the headquarters for the cause of beatification.

The beautifully prepared exhibition included photos of various events and people involved with the apparitions. Carlo listened intently to the testimony of one of the sisters from Lisbon, whose grandfather was present at the miracle of the sun on October 13, 1917: a miracle that was also visible in the surrounding areas. Carlo was dumbfounded by everything he had seen and heard. He had previously learned of Sister Lucia's diary containing the four memoirs. He brought it with him to read during a trip to France with his parents. When he got to the part where the three *pastorelli* asked Our Lady if they would be taken up into heaven, and she responded that Lucia and Jacinta definitely would be, but that

Francesco would have to recite a lot of rosaries, Carlo was quite worried. In fact, he said to his parents, "If a goodhearted, simple kid like Francesco had to recite so many rosaries to get to heaven, what chance do I have?" Then when Carlo read that the children had asked Our Lady where a recently deceased friend of theirs named Amalia was, the Virgin's response troubled him: "She will be in purgatory until the end of the ages" because she loved dancing too much. Carlo asked his parents a lot of questions after this and reflected on it for a long time. He became even more worried when he read the account of their vision of hell: "Our Lady showed us a great sea of fire which seemed to be under the earth. Plunged in this fire were demons and souls in human form, like transparent burning embers, all blackened or burnished bronze, floating about in the conflagration, now raised into the air by the flames that issued from within themselves together with great clouds of smoke, now falling back on every side like sparks in a huge fire, without weight or equilibrium, and amid shrieks and groans of pain and despair, which horrified us and made us tremble with fear. The demons could be distinguished by their terrifying and repulsive likeness to frightful and unknown animals, all black and transparent." Reading this account made Carlo pray even harder for those who risked losing their souls in eternal damnation.

Carlo also wanted to visit La Loca do Cabeço, the place where the three children had a vision of an angel who identified himself as the guardian angel of Portugal and administered the Holy Eucharist to them. In a biography of Jacinta written by her cousin, Sister Lucia dos Santos, Servant of God, we read: "I think it must have been in the spring of 1916 that the Angel appeared to us for the first time in our Loca do Cabeço. As I have already written in my account of Jacinta, we climbed the hillside in search of shelter. After having taken our lunch and said our prayers, we began to see, some distance off, above the trees that stretched away towards the east, a light, whiter than snow, in the form of a young man, transparent, and brighter than crystal pierced by the rays of the sun. As he drew nearer, we could distinguish his features more and more clearly. We were surprised, absorbed, and struck dumb with amazement. On reaching us, he said: 'Do not be afraid. I am the Angel of Peace. Pray with me.' Kneeling on the ground, he bowed down until his forehead touched the earth. Led by a supernatural impulse, we did the same, and repeated the words which we heard him say: 'My God, I believe, I adore, I hope and I love You! I ask pardon of You for those who do not believe, do not adore, do not hope and do not love You!' Having repeated these words three times, he rose and said: 'Pray thus. The Hearts of Jesus and Mary are attentive to the voice of your supplications.' Then he disappeared. The supernatural atmosphere which enveloped us was so intense, that we were for a long time scarcely aware of our own existence, remaining in the same posture in which he had left us, and continually repeating the same prayer. The presence of God made itself felt so intimately and so intensely that we did not even venture to speak to one another. Next day, we were still immersed in this spiritual atmosphere, which only gradually began to disappear. It did not occur to us to speak about this Apparition, nor did we think of recommending that it be kept secret. The very Apparition itself imposed secrecy. It was so intimate, that it was not easy to speak of it at all. The impression it made upon us was all the greater perhaps, in that it was the first such manifestation that we had experienced. The second Apparition must have been at the height of summer, when the heat of the day was so intense that we had to take the sheep home before noon and only let them out again in the early evening.

We went to spend the siesta hours in the shade of the trees which surrounded the well that I have already mentioned several times. Suddenly, we saw the same Angel right beside us. 'What are you doing?' he asked. 'Pray! Pray very much! The Hearts of Jesus and Mary have designs of mercy on you. Offer prayers and sacrifices constantly to the Most High.' 'How are we to make sacrifices?' I asked. 'Make of everything you can a sacrifice, and offer it to God as an act of reparation for the sins by which He is offended, and in supplication for the conversion of sinners. You will thus draw down peace upon your country. I am its Angel Guardian, the Angel of Portugal. Above all, accept and bear with submission, the suffering which the Lord will send you.' These words were indelibly impressed upon our minds. They were like a light which made us understand who God is, how He loves us and desires to be loved, the value of sacrifice, how pleasing it is to Him and how, on account of it, He grants the grace of conversion to sinners. It was for this reason that we began, from then on, to offer to the Lord all that mortified us."

Carlo interpreted one particular detail of the Fatima apparitions that left everyone stunned. He explained the third secret in an allegorical way, saying it could be interpreted in light of the Eucharist, because "the cross on the mountain can also represent the sacrifice of Christ who gives himself for the salvation of men, celebrated in every Mass. The blood that the angels collected under his arms and sprinkled the faithful with as they struggled to climb the mountain is the Blood that the Lord pours out in every Eucharistic celebration on the human race, together with the blood of the martyrs who purify and clean the hearts of men from their sins. The arrows that strike the faithful as they climb toward the summit could symbolize all the difficulties human beings face as they strive to merit heaven. The figure of a bishop dressed in white has already been associated with John Paul II, as the Church has explained. John Paul always insisted on the importance of the Eucharist and was himself a 'martyr.' This further clarifies the Eucharistic meaning of the vision."

It was from his devotion to Our Lady of Fatima that Carlo adopted the practice of observing the First Saturdays of the month in accord with what Sister Lucia wrote in 1925. The Virgin asked all men and women to console her and to make reparation for offenses committed against her Immaculate Heart, promising that "anyone who goes to Confession on the First Saturday for five consecutive months and receives Holy Communion, recites the Rosary, and keeps company with me for fifteen minutes meditating on the mysteries with the intention of offering reparation for sins, will be assisted by me in the hour of death with all the graces necessary for salvation."

The eternal destiny of his soul was something that concerned Carlo greatly. He saw heaven as the goal toward which to apply all his efforts. To orient himself so as to never lose sight of the goal, he used an infallible compass: the Bible. For Carlo, the Word of God was a light in the midst of the fog, a beacon in the stormy seas of life on this world. This is why prayer and the sacraments became the indispensable means offered by God to reach the desired goal.

Carlo was deeply impressed when Saint John Paul II – surrounded by bishops from all over the world — consecrated the new millennium to Our Lady in the Great Jubilee Year of 2000. Carlo himself was present for the event. He was particularly moved by the presence of the statue of Our Lady of Fatima in the middle of Saint Peter's Square after it arrived all the way from Portugal. Carlo always had great respect for all the successors of Peter. He was very attentive to the teaching of the Magisterium and the Roman Pontiff. He always responded readily to the appeals to prayer and fasting that John Paul II and Benedict XVI made to the faithful on several occasions. He had a deep love for the pope and the Church: His final sufferings before death were offered for them. This offering of sacrifice was in response to the appeals of Our Lady of Fatima to the shepherd children and the entire Church to pray and make sacrifices for sinners and the pope.

THE SAINTS

Besides the Virgin Mary, Carlo also practiced a deep veneration for all the saints. He particularly loved Saint Francis, whose life he learned thoroughly during multiple pilgrimages to Assisi.

Carlo was deeply struck by the humility of the Poverello, who continually wanted to decrease so that Christ might increase in him. Carlo often told his parents of the need to become humble and feel we are "nothing" if we wish to become true disciples of the Master. But he also warned that it is not enough to consider ourselves "humble" if all we do is be kind and charitable to our neighbor. He was convinced that humility was one of the most difficult virtues to obtain: "We all are likely to fall short because as soon as someone says something we don't like, we instantly grow angry." Carlo was amazed at Saint Francis' love for the Eucharist and zeal to teach everyone the Gospel. Remembering the sacrifices and the penances of the Poverello, Carlo was able to overcome his tendency toward gluttony, thus purifying his one peccadillo. During his trips to Assisi, he loved to walk the *Via Crucis* in the footsteps of his beloved saint. He also made a point to visit other places important to the Franciscan tradition, such as the shrine at La Verna, where Francis received the stigmata from the seraph during the feast of the Exaltation of the Cross in 1224. Carlo loved to go to La Verna for various courses and spiritual retreats. He was fascinated by the saint's complete giving of himself to Christ, the humility with which he overcame every passion, and the fire of love he had in God's presence, especially in the Eucharist.

There was one passage about the Eucharist written by Saint Francis particularly dear to Carlo: "Behold: Daily he humbles himself as when from heaven's royal throne he came down into the womb of the Virgin. Daily he himself comes to us with like humility. Daily he descends from the bosom of the Father upon the altar in the hands of the priest. And as he appeared to the apostles in true flesh, so now also he shows himself to us in the sacred bread. And as they by their bodily sight saw only his flesh, yet contemplating him with the eyes of the spirit believed him to be God, so we also, as we see with our bodily eyes the bread and wine, are to see and firmly believe that it is his most holy Body and Blood living and true. And in this way the Lord is always with his faithful, as he himself says: Behold I am with you until the end of the world."

Saint Francis is also the patron of ecology, the protector of the environment, the home common to us all, as Pope Francis emphasized in his encyclical *Laudato Si'* published on May 24, 2015. The pope explains why he chose the name of Francis as his guide and inspiration when he was elected Bishop of Rome. "I believe that Saint Francis is the example *par excellence* of care for the vulnerable and of an integral ecology lived out joyfully and authentically. He is the patron saint of all who study and work in the area of ecology, and he is also much loved by non-Christians."

In fact, Saint Francis "was particularly concerned for God's creation and for the poor and outcast. He loved, and was deeply loved for his joy, his generous self-giving, his openheartedness. He was a mystic and a pilgrim who lived in simplicity and in wonderful harmony with God, with others, with nature and with himself. He shows us just how insepa-rable the bond is between concern for nature, justice for the poor, commitment to society, and interior peace." The witness of the Poverello, Pope Francis explained, also shows that an integral ecology "calls for openness to categories which tran-scend the language of mathematics and biology, and take us to the heart of what it is to be human." Just as happens when we fall in love with someone, whenever he would gaze at the sun, the moon or the smallest of animals, he burst into song, drawing all other creatures into his praise. He communed with all creation, even preaching to the flowers, inviting them 'to praise the Lord, just as if they were endowed with reason.'" Carlo also had a special regard for the environment, and his attitude exemplifies the teaching of Pope Francis in the encyc-lical. His love for creation was, in fact, so strong that he bought himself a special walking stick to collect trash whenever he went on hikes in the mountains or walked along the seashore.

Carlo also had a deep love for Anthony of Padua. He con-sidered him a great preacher of the Word, an evangelizer, and an apostle for the Eucharist. He was particularly struck by the story of Saint Anthony converting a heretic in Rimini who did not believe that Jesus was truly present in the Eucharist. When Anthony showed the consecrated host to a mule, the beast got down on its knees. Anthony then told the heretic, "The animal must certainly have been inspired by the Lord to refute the unbelief of most people since he certainly would have preferred a bale of hay than to adore the Lord." Padua, too, became a special place for Carlo to visit. He begged his parents to take him there so that he could pray to the saint whom he considered a model of Eucharistic piety and a true missionary.

Carlo's admiration for Francis and Anthony enflamed his desire to imitate their charity, especially toward the poor. Every day he strove to become more generous. Once, while walking with his dogs in the woods near Assisi, he saw a beggar sleeping on the ground in a public park. He continued to see him there regularly, so he asked his parents to prepare something to eat that he could take to him. Then he went to take it to him and left him a euro as well. He did the same with the homeless who often slept on a church step near his home in Milan. He often brought some of his supper to them. He once saved enough money to buy a sleeping bag for one of them who had been sleeping on cardboard boxes. Any time he was able, Carlo tried to help the poor in whatever way he could. Two homeless persons gave this testimony: "I came to know Carlo Acutis because he always went to daily Mass. ... Because I was out of work, I found myself begging for alms on the steps of the Church of Santa Maria Segreta. I remember Carlo well. He was always so kind, good-hearted, and well-mannered. Every once in a while he would give me some money, which I believe came from his allowance. There aren't too many kids around like Carlo these days."

Another said: "I got to know Carlo Acutis because I often begged in front of the Church of Santa Maria Segreta. I saw Carlo coming to Mass every day either at 6:00 p.m. or at 7:00 p.m. He often gave me part of his allowance, and he always stopped to talk to me for a while and encourage me. I remember his kindness, generosity, and his enormous faith. Once, when a friend I had met at the homeless shelter named Giuseppina refused to eat or drink because of severe depression and resigned herself to die in the piazza in front of the church, no one but Carlo, his mother, and I showed any interest in helping her. Carlo and his mother were able to admit her to the Fatebenefratelli hospital, where she stayed for forty days in recovery. No one in this neighborhood ever showed any interest in me except Carlo. He was really too good and pure for this world, and I will never forget him."

Carlo was convinced that God had a special love for the poor, and he often said, "Those who enjoy a high income or have a string of noble titles after their names should not boast or think they are better than others." Carlo had a deep respect for the inviolable dignity of every human being, be they of noble stock or be they a street dweller. He used to say, "Noble titles and money mean so little. What really counts in life is the nobility of soul or the manner in which we love God and neighbor." He had no patience for inequality and injustice because "all men and women are created by God."

On fire with apostolic zeal, Carlo also tried to help the Christian missions in any way he could. For example, Capuchin Father Giulio Savoldi, vice-postulator and confessor of the Servant of God, Brother Cecilio Maria Cortinovis — a doorman and founder of a soup kitchen in Milan that distributed about five thousand meals a day — shares this memory of Carlo's mindfulness toward those most in need: "I had the fortune of meeting Carlo on various occasions. He was serene, bright faced, enthusiastic about anything good and beautiful, and clearly full of the Holy Spirit. He was eager to meet the needs of the poor, the suffering, and the less fortunate in any way he could, especially by assuaging their pain. Once, he brought me his entire piggy bank to give to kids who needed it more. He was always ready to encourage his peers when they were down, instilling faith and confidence in them and putting a smile on their faces as they received strength to assume their responsibilities. Carlo was not prone to judge or to blame anyone making a mistake. Rather, he eagerly rushed to help troubled souls find serenity and peace in the way of Jesus, sent by the Father not to condemn but to save. I thank the Good Lord for the opportunity to have gotten to know him. Personally, I feel his presence as a guide to live faithfully in my vocation according to the mysterious designs of the God, full of goodness and mercy."

In addition to the saints, Carlo made a habit of praying to the angels. In 2004, during a pilgrimage to the Shrine of the Rosary in Pompei, his mother took him to visit the convent of Padre Pio in San Giovanni Rotondo. They were given a ride by a taxi driver who had been a spiritual son of the saint. He told them that Padre Pio often asked him to bring people troubled by demons directly to the Shrine of Saint Michael in Gargano. "Only there," the saint said, "is it possible to obtain healing of soul and body." We can imagine that Carlo immediately asked his mother to take him to the shrine. One of the guides explained to them that the depth of the grotto represented the need for the pilgrims to Saint Michael to make a journey deep into themselves to purify their sins and rise again healed. Carlo was overcome with emotion when he learned that the archangel left one of his footprints on the rock. From that day onward, Carlo began to recite the angelic chaplet dedicated to the nine choirs of angels. This chaplet is divided into twenty-seven Hail Marys and nine Our Fathers, dedicated to each group of angels. According to tradition, this chaplet was revealed directly by Saint Michael to Portuguese Servant of God Antonia de Astonac.

THE APOSTOLATE

Animated by the zeal Carlo saw reflected in the examples of the saints he loved so much, he prayed not only for sinners but also for non-Christians, beginning with the Jews to whom he felt especially close. Carlo completed a school research project on them using a program exclusive to professionals. He said that "the biggest gift that God made to men was to send his only Son, Jesus Christ," and for this reason Carlo was very sad that so many had not yet met him. This is why he saw how necessary it was to preach the Gospel, as he said: "It is very important to pray that Jesus Christ be loved and known by all peoples throughout the world." Carlo placed much emphasis on interreligious dialogue, because he considered it a privileged moment to let others know what we believe and what the teachings of the Gospel are. This is why he closely followed on television the interreligious gathering in Assisi that John Paul II presided over on January 24, 2002.

Carlo said the following about the event: "With these inter-religious meetings, the pope gives everyone the possibility of knowing and loving Jesus Christ, the one Savior of the world upon whom the salvation of all human beings depends."

Through relationships with people like custodians in his neighborhood and domestic help, Carlo was in constant contact with people of other religions, especially Buddhists and Hindus. He learned as much as he could about them and prayed that adherents to these religions would come to know Jesus Christ. He used to say that "the Gospel needs to be proclaimed to all peoples, just as Jesus Christ taught."

As already mentioned, Carlo was very close to Rajesh, who offered domestic help to Carlo and his family and who knew Carlo since Carlo was four. Carlo treated him like a playmate and a confidant, calling him, "my trusty friend Rajesh." He always included Rajesh in the short films he made. Rajesh would often play the role of a James-Bond-type international spy.

Rajesh left one of the most important testimonies of Carlo's life: "Considering how deep Carlo's faith was, it was normal that he offer me lessons in the Catholic religion, even though I am of the Hindu Brahmin priestly class. Carlo said that I would have a happier future if I grew close to Jesus, and he often taught me with Scripture, the *Catechism*, and stories about the saints. He practically knew the *Catechism of the Catholic Church* by heart, and his explanations were so brilliant that he was able to get me very excited about the importance of the sacraments. He had a talent for explaining theological concepts in a way that not even adults could explain. Gradually, I began to take his counsel and teaching more seriously until I finally decided to be baptized a Christian." Rajesh continues, "Carlo taught me how to live the Christian life authentically. He was an outstanding example of moral uprightness. I decided to be baptized because Carlo deeply and directly influenced me with his profound faith, his broad charity, and his sense of purity, which I always considered exceptional, because a boy as young, handsome, and wealthy as Carlo usually lives a very different life. Carlo is such a high example of spirituality and holiness that I felt deep within me the desire to be baptized a Christian and to receive Holy Communion. He explained to me the importance of receiving daily Communion and to pray to the Virgin Mary in the Rosary, striving to internalize the heroic virtues. Carlo also used to say: 'Virtue is acquired primarily through an intense sacramental life, and the Eucharist is undoubtedly the culmination of charity. Through this sacrament the Lord makes us be complete persons, created in his image,' and he would add words from the sixth chapter of the Gospel of John that he had memorized: 'He who eats my flesh and drinks my blood has eternal life, and I will raise him up on the last day.' Then he would explain to me that the Eucharist was the heart of Christ. Once, he also told me the importance of practicing the First Friday devotion to the Sacred Heart and the First Saturday devotion to the Immaculate Heart of Mary. He also said that 'the Heart of Jesus and the Heart of Mary are indissolubly joined, and when we receive Communion we come into direct contact with Our Lady and the saints in heaven. God is extremely pleased by the souls that approach the great gifts of the Eucharist and the Sacrament of Confession.'"

Rajesh also remembers how Carlo prepared him to receive the Sacrament of Confirmation and explained to him its importance. Carlo said that when he received the sacrament, he felt a mysterious power inside of him that he cherished, and which he felt grow through his Eucharistic devotion. Rajesh recounted that when he received the Sacrament of Confirmation, he felt the same thing.

What struck Rajesh the most was Carlo's extraordinary purity and faithfulness to daily Mass. Carlo had such a bright vision of the Catholic faith. Everyone was infected by the serenity and sweetness with which he presented the truth of the Catholic Faith.

Other non-Christians have testified to Carlo's faith. Many found Carlo to be a shining example of virtue inspiring everyone to reflect on their own values, integrity of life, simplicity, and coherence with what they believed. Carlo's life reflected the depth of his faith in a clear, transparent way.

EPILOGUE

Despite the brevity Carlo's life, he was ready to pass over definitively from this life into heaven. At the beginning of 2006, he fell ill with symptoms that seemed to be nothing but the common flu. Yet it turned out to be M3-type leukemia, which doctors consider the most aggressive form, almost impossible to heal. His personal physician, as well as a family friend who was a doctor, first thought it was the mumps. His parents recall that a few days before he was admitted to the hospital, while they were keeping vigil at his bedside, they heard Carlo say: "I offer all the sufferings that I will have to undergo to the Lord for the pope and the Church, so that I can avoid purgatory and go straight to heaven."

At first, his parents didn't think much of this affirmation, but as the days passed, they realized how prophetic it was.

His parents also remember how they would always draw a name of a saint from a hat on the evening of December

31 according to an ancient Milanese custom. His family was always amazed that Carlo would draw the most important saints such as the Holy Family, Jesus, or Mary, and they would tease him saying that he was always receiving the "highest recommendations." Then, in 2006, he drew the name of Saint Alexander Sauli, a Barnabite bishop, patron of young students, whose feast was celebrated on October 11 — the exact day on which Carlo would die. Even more strangely, the clinic where Carlo was first treated was right across the street from a Barnabite Church in which the remains of Saint Alexander Sauli were kept. His parents immediately understood that this could not be a coincidence, but only a sign of God's plan.

Carlo's apparent "flu" really began to trouble his parents, especially since, four days later, Carlo found blood in his urine after waking up. His mother called the doctor, who told her to bring a sample of his urine into the laboratory for testing to see if there might be a urinary tract infection. The test turned out negative, but Carlo's health was not getting any better. He was extremely weak on Sunday morning, so his parents called his pediatric doctor, who had known him for years. This doctor recommended checking him into the De Marchi clinic of which he was the director, and which also happened to specialize in childrens' blood diseases.

As soon as they got to the hospital, the doctors realized the gravity of the situation and informed his parents that his chances of survival were extremely slim. Just like any parents, his father and mother could hardly accept that their son would soon be dead. In accord with the law, the chief of the hematology department at the clinic had to inform Carlo that he had leukemia and that any hope for a cure would take a very long time. Once the doctor left the room, Carlo remained serene and composed: "The Lord has given me a wake-up call!"

Within hours, he was transferred to intensive care where a plastic helmet was placed on his head to facilitate breathing. This instrument, however, was extremely uncomfortable and caused a lot of suffering, because whenever he coughed, he was unable to expel his mucus. His mother asked to stay with him in the intensive care unit until 1:00 in the morning. After that time, he remained alone with the helmet on, completely unable to sleep. He was anxiously awaiting the morning when he could see his mother again, who had stayed in the hospital the entire night with his grandmother Luana so that she could be on hand for any emergency. The doctor who had care for him decided to transfer him to San Gerardo Hospital in Monza where there is a special care unit for children with the type of leukemia that Carlo was suffering from. There, his mother and grandmother were able to sleep in the same room with him. Carlo considered that a godsend. His parents asked a priest to administer the Sacrament of the Anointing of the Sick to him.

The nurses and doctors taking care of Carlo at that time were struck by his behavior and his willingness to accept the pain of his illness without ever complaining. He always kept a smile on his face. They considered him the bravest kid they had ever met. He never wanted to show his suffering. In the last night of his illness, he was afraid that his mother was not sleeping enough, or that the nurses would tire trying to change his position since he was too tall. One of the female doctors asked Carlo if he was suffering a lot, because doctors consider M3 to be one of the most painful forms of leukemia. But with a smile, Carlo disarmingly responded: "There are a lot of people suffering much more than me." He was thinking of others all the way to the very end, because that was his style. His legs and arms were terribly inflated with liquid. After he returned from his CAT scan, the nurses jokingly asked him if he were feeling better. With a smile, he responded: "Yes."

The next day, at 2:00 p.m., the nurses were putting him in his protective suit, and the doctor asked him once more how he was doing. As always, he said, "Well." Within half an hour, he had fallen into a coma. He was moved to the intensive care unit where he was administered a special blood infusion to separate his red blood cells from his white blood cells. The procedure went well. But within a short amount of time, he was overcome by a cerebral hemorrhage and died. His bodily organs had been so compromised that he could not even donate them. The doctors decided not to remove his respirator until his heart stopped beating on its own. He was declared brain dead on October 11, 2006, but his heart stopped beating at 6:45 a.m. on October 12, the vigil of the last apparition at Fatima. The testimony of those who were near him in his last moments agree that his acceptance of death was truly a manifest expression of a sanctity that could only derive from a profound interior life and a special mystical experience.

News of Carlo's death immediately circulated among his friends and classmates at the Istituto Tommaseo and Leone XIII. His parents were given permission to have his body brought home, where it was arranged in his bedroom. For the four days during which the coffin remained open, there was a constant line of mourners visiting. Many sensed a perfume of lilies coming from his body.

The funeral was celebrated in the church of Santa Maria Segreta on October 14, 2006. A crowd of people participated, such that many were unable to enter the building. Among these were many immigrants who were personal friends of Carlo belonging to a variety of religions whom his family had never met before. The liturgical rite did not appear so much a funeral as a festival. When the priest had finished the ceremony, gave the blessing, and said, "Go in peace," those in attendance heard festive bells because the ceremony happened to finish right when the noon bells were ringing. The celebrating priests considered this a sign that Carlo was in heaven and in the presence of Christ. He was buried in the family tomb in Ternengo (Biella), and from there his remains were transferred to the cemetery in Assisi in 2007.

After the unexpected and sudden loss of their son, his parents asked themselves whether Carlo had some sense of his imminent death. Some weeks after his passing, his mother found a video that had been filmed two months prior. In the film, Carlo said, "I have put on seventy kilograms and I am destined to die." Carlo must have realized that his existence on this earth would be brief, because he also had a sixth sense that allowed him to anticipate events before they happened.

But Carlo's death did not mark the end of his presence on earth. His memory lives on in the minds and hearts of everyone who knew him. Many people pray to him with faith and seek his intercession, convinced that he died in a state of grace and showed every sign of being a true disciple of Christ.

Over the course of the years, his life and message have spread throughout the world. Parishes have dedicated retreats and days of reflection to his legacy. Youth groups and lay associations have read his biography and reflected on his earthly life and on his indissoluble link with Christ. Schools — such as a high school in France — and clubs have named themselves after him, not to mention prayer groups for young people created across the globe to follow his spirituality. A witness to the Gospel, Carlo was a burning light for so many of his peers who opened their lives to his teaching and seek to live an integral life of Christian faith.

Carlo's exhibits have traveled to many countries. They have been requested by parishes, religious institutions, and lay associations. These exhibits, which are both artistic and historical, are most of all an expression of faith and have enjoyed enormous success. The four that have been most remarkable are: "Eucharistic Miracles throughout the World," "Our Lady's Appeals, Apparitions, and Shrines throughout the World," "Angels and Demons," and "Hell, Purgatory, and Heaven."

Thousands of letters, messages, and requests for books and materials arrive via email and post to his parents and the Association of Friends of Carlo Acutis, the latter of which was established to promote his spirituality and to promote his cause of beatification. The Association is also dedicated to various charitable works such as the building of an orphanage in collaboration with the bishops of Tanzania and the "Christians in the World" Association. All this is done in the memory and name of Carlo.

It is truly astounding how quickly Carlo's reputation and legacy have spread through the world. Hundreds of graces have been received through his intercession. And all this without any concerted effort to spread his reputation. It was all spontaneous. But it could not have been otherwise, considering that the area in which Carlo most excelled was in computer programming. Many of Carlo's friends first met him on the internet. Many have been fascinated with his life and faith precisely by discovering his story on the internet. An initial encounter with him quickly leads to further discovery of his message and his life. There are many — not just young people — who are amazed by his discipleship and cannot remain indifferent to their own faith life. His example invites us to change our lives and reflect. His message was also very present at World Youth Day in Rio de Janeiro in July of 2013.

His enduring fame and holiness have inspired the Diocese of Milan to promote his cause of beatification and canonization, which opened on October 12, 2012. The *nulla osta* for his cause was issued by the Congregation for the Causes of Saints on May 13, 2013. After a delay due to the COVID-19 pandemic, Carlo was finally beatified at the Basilica of Saint Francis of Assisi in Assisi on October 10, 2020. Crowds of pilgrims have never ceased to flock to his tomb since.